Authorized By No Law

United States Circuit Judge Matthew Hall McAllister. (Courtesy Archives, United States District Court for the Northern District of California.)

Authorized By No Law

The San Francisco
Committee of Vigilance
of 1856

and the

United States Circuit Court
for the Districts of California

by

John D. Gordan, III

Published by

Ninth Judicial Circuit Historical Society
Pasadena

and

United States District Court for the
Northern District of California Historical Society
San Francisco

1987

Copyright © 1985 by John D. Gordan, III

Library of Congress Cataloging-in Publication Data

Gordan, John D., 1945-
  Authorized by no law.

  1. Criminal justice, Administration of—California—History. 2. Circuit courts—California—History.
3. Maritime law—United States—History. 4. Pirates—California—San Francisco—History. 5. San Francisco Committee of Vigilance of 1856. I. Title.
KFC1102.G67 1987   345.794'05'09   87-21986
ISBN 0-9618731-0-8   347.9405509

Back cover picture courtesy California State Libary.

Printed in the United States of America.

ISBN 0-9618731-0-8

Preface

In "Twenty-Four Years After," the chapter added to *Two Years Before the Mast* after a trip to San Francisco in 1859, Richard Henry Dana, Jr., wrote:

> But it [San Francisco] has been through its season of Heaven-defying crime, violence and blood, from which it was rescued and handed back to soberness, morality and good government, by that peculiar invention of Anglo-Saxon Republican America, the solemn, awe-inspiring Vigilance Committee of the most grave and responsible citizens, the last resort of the thinking and the good, taken to only when vice, fraud and ruffianism have intrenched themselves behind the forms of law, suffrage, and ballot, and there is no hope but in organized force, whose action must be instant and thorough, or its state will be worse than before. A history of the passage of this city through those ordeals, and through its almost incredible financial extremes, should be written by a pen which not only accuracy shall govern, but imagination shall inspire.

Dana's call has since been answered by many historians, whose writings are analyzed in an appendix to the most recent treatment of San Francisco's Committees of Vigilance, Robert M. Senkewicz, S.J., *Vigilantes in Gold Rush San Francisco* (Stanford, 1985). The role of the courts of the United States in these events has not, however, been considered to any significant extent.

The limited narrative which follows is not an effort to fill this gap in any comprehensive way, nor to deal broadly with the purposes and deeds of the Vigilance Committee of 1856. My intention instead is to examine the administration of justice in the federal courts in circumstances which are in many ways historically unique.

The happiest part of this endeavor is to express my thanks to those who have made it possible. The first of these is Professor Christian G. Fritz, the leading authority on the federal courts in 19th century California and the author of a comprehensive biography, recently completed, of Judge Ogden Hoffman of the United States District Court for the Northern District of California. His help in providing crucial materials I would never otherwise have found, his insights into the history of California's early federal courts, and his generous and patient encouragement account for much of whatever here may be of interest or value to the reader. Of great assistance, too, were Joseph Franaszek, Esq., Assistant Circuit Executive of the United States Court of Appeals for the Ninth Circuit, and Dr. Michael Griffith, archivist of the United States District Court for the Northern District of California, both of whom kindly supplied material and enthusiasm indispensable to this undertaking. Finally, I want to thank the Ninth Judicial Circuit Historical Society and the United States District Court for the Northern District of California Historical Society for their support in publishing this book.

John D. Gordan, III

Authorized By No Law

INTRODUCTION

On June 21, 1856, two hours after midnight, while at anchor in San Pablo Bay fifteen miles northeast of San Francisco, the schooner *Julia* was boarded by an armed party sent to seize her cargo of muskets by the executive committee of the San Francisco Vigilance Committee, the governing body of the group of several thousand citizens who had risen to seize control of the city five weeks before. Before the day ended, the commissioner of the United States Circuit Court for the Districts of California had issued warrants for the arrest of three of the boarding party on charges of piracy, while the leader of those they had surprised aboard the *Julia*, James Reuben Molony, lay in cell no. 1 at Fort Vigilance, the headquarters of the Vigilance Committee on Sacramento Street, more popularly called "Fort Gunnybags" after its principal fortification.

Down the corridor from Molony the Honorable David S. Terry, associate justice of the Supreme Court of California, was locked in cell no. 8. His efforts that afternoon to prevent Molony's recapture by the Vigilance Committee had begun with a running battle in the streets of San Francisco, during which the justice used the Bowie knife he habitually carried to inflict an apparently fatal wound upon one of the committee's policemen, and had ended with the committee's successful siege of the armory in which both had taken refuge.

The events of June 21, 1856 and their aftermath illuminate a season — the July 1856 term — in the brief existence of a unique but forgotten court to which only one, equally unremembered judge was ever appointed — the United States Circuit Court for the Districts of California.[1] The boarding of the *Julia* would confront the court in that term with the first occasion to consider the application of the federal piracy statute to domestic insurrection, an issue which, in jurisprudentially different circumstances, would several times recur during the Civil War.[2] It provides today an opportunity to observe the federal judicial process at a time and in a place where supremacy lay with the judged, and not with the judges.

I
THE COURT AND THE JUDGE

The creation of the United States Circuit Court for the Districts of California was part of a two-decade effort by the United States to digest California's statehood judicially. An understanding of the uniqueness of that court requires some reference to the evolution of the judicial system of the United States following the adoption of the Constitution.

The United States circuit courts existed from the creation of the federal judiciary by the Judiciary Act of 1789.[3] They were, until the Evarts Act of 1891,[4] the federal courts of general first instance jurisdiction, with appellate jurisdiction of the judgments of the district courts, also established by the Judiciary Act of 1789 to hear cases in admiralty and try minor criminal offenses. Originally each United States circuit court was composed of two itinerant justices of the Supreme Court of the United States and the district judge of the district for which the circuit court was held; in 1793, the number of Supreme Court justices required to sit with the district judge was reduced to one.[5]

In 1801, to relieve the Supreme Court justices of their arduous circuit-riding duties and allegedly to perpetuate Federalist dominance of the judiciary, the Sixth Congress passed and President Adams signed the Judiciary Act of 1801, which replaced the existing system with six circuits, each, except the Sixth, the jurisdiction of a United States circuit court composed of three United States circuit judges.[6] The circuit judges appointed under the act in the last days of President Adams' administration came to be known in history as the "midnight judges."

These courts had existed for only one year when they were abolished by the Judiciary Act of 1802, nearly the first order of business of the new administration of President Thomas Jefferson.[7] The United States circuit judges, despite the provisions of Article III of the United States Constitution, were deprived of their offices and salaries with the acquiescence of the Supreme Court, *Stuart v. Laird*, 1 Cranch (5 U.S.) 299 (1803), although the private opinions of some of the justices were quite the opposite of their published one.[8] The former circuit court system of Supreme Court justices and district judges was restored by the Judiciary Act of 1802 and continued until 1869.

As the nation expanded westward, the judicial power of the United States in the marches time and again vested in United States district courts which, because of remoteness from the itinerary of any eastern circuit-riding Supreme Court justice, also exercised the jurisdiction of the United States circuit courts. The first such courts were established by the Judiciary Act of 1789 in "that part of the state of Massachusetts which lies easterly of the state of New Hampshire," known as "Main," and in Kentucky, then part of Virginia. After California was admitted to the Union, a similar arrangement was established there by the "Act to provide for extending the Laws and the Judicial System of the United States to the State of California," enacted in September 1850.[9] That statute created district courts for the northern and southern districts of California and conferred upon the single judge of each, with proper deference to the nation's first district court, the "same jurisdiction and powers which were by law given to the judge of the southern district of New York." Section 10 of the act, and the Act of February 26, 1853,[10] additionally conferred upon these district courts the jurisdiction and powers "now exercised by the Circuit Courts of the United States." Judge Ogden Hoffman was appointed to the northern district bench in 1851 and held that position for the next forty years. The southern district judgeship, when not vacant, was filled from time to time with men of limited stature; from 1852 to 1854 and for twenty years beginning in 1866, it was abolished altogether.

The most significant business of both district courts and principally of Judge Hoffman, who was obliged by the absence of a southern district judge from 1851 to 1854 to hold the district court alone in both districts, was to review decisions of the Board of Land Commissioners under the "Act to ascertain and settle the private Land Claims in the State of California" (March 3, 1851).[11] The volume of business under that statute, the physical impossibility of the discharge of circuit duties in such a remote location by a justice of the Supreme Court also required to sit in Washington, the necessity of a circuit court to provide a means for local appellate review of the district court and the possibility of review in the Supreme Court in criminal cases, and the continuing absence of Judge Hoffman in New York on account of illness, beginning in August, 1854, led to the introduction in the Senate, on February 5, 1855, of a bill to establish the United States Circuit Court for the Districts of California.[12] The bill passed the Senate a week later, was approved by the House on February 27, and signed into law on March 2, 1855. The only serious opposition in Congress had come from Louisiana Senator Judah P. Benjamin, who, in 1850, had declined his commission as the first United States district judge for the northern district of California. He pronounced himself and many other senators entirely opposed to

> the introduction of any system by which circuit courts shall be established to perform circuit duties, and to entertain circuit court jurisdiction, to the relief of the Judges of the Supreme Court of the United States, so as eventually to constitute the Supreme Court a local court, isolated in Washington, and kept separate from circuit duties.[13]

The "Act to establish a Circuit Court of the United States in and for the State of California"[14] created a court with the original jurisdiction of the circuit courts and appellate jurisdiction over the district courts in the northern and southern districts, to be exercised at a single term of court to be held annually at San Francisco on the first Monday of July and such other terms there as the circuit judge might appoint. Section 6 of the act provided that whenever either district court was to sit in review of decisions of the Board of Land Commissioners under the Act of March 3, 1851, the clerk of the district court must notify the circuit judge, who had discretion to preside in the district court in such cases or, if the district judge were absent, to hold the district court alone.

The act provided for the appointment of a judge of the court, and on the day it became law, President Franklin Pierce nominated Matthew Hall McAllister as the

United States circuit judge, the first since the ill-fated judges under the Judiciary Act of 1801, his only predecessors, the last until the Act of 1869 and the only one ever appointed to hold the United States Circuit Court for the Districts of California.[15] The Senate confirmed the nomination by a unanimous vote the next day.[16]

Judge McAllister was born in Savannah, Georgia, in 1800, the son of a judge of the Georgia Superior Court. He attended college at Princeton and in 1827 was appointed United States district attorney for the southern district of Georgia. Later he served several terms as mayor of Savannah, was elected to the Georgia state senate, and in 1845 narrowly lost the election for governor of Georgia as the candidate of the Democratic party. In addition to his law practice, Judge McAllister was a landowner, rice planter and slaveholder.[17]

In 1849 one of his several sons, Hall, began a notable career as a trial lawyer in San Francisco. He promptly wrote back to Savannah urging his father to join him in practice in San Francisco, pointing out that, although an acknowledged leader of the Georgia bar, it took his father a year to earn what Hall could earn in two months. Judge McAllister's first reaction, according to his son Ward, was: "It is hard for an old tree to take root in a new soil."[18] But Hall's dispatch of a quantity of gold dust to Ward, coupled with Judge McAllister's receipt of a five thousand dollar fee as counsel in *Kennedy v. Bank of the State of Georgia*, 49 U.S. 586 (1850), enabled Ward to persuade his father to move to San Francisco. Judge McAllister closed his practice, sold his house and in May 1850 set out with his family for San Francisco.[19]

Once there, Judge McAllister and Ward went into partnership with Hall. Although the cost of living was beyond belief, so were the fees. Ward McAllister reports that the new firm's first retainer was four thousand dollars in gold coin, and "as I laid them ounce by ounce on my father's desk, he danced a pirouette, for he was as jolly an old fellow as ever lived."[20] The firm earned a hundred thousand dollars a year.[21] After two years, Judge McAllister had accumulated a comfortable fortune and retired from practice. He and Ward left San Francisco, Ward to live in New York and his father in Europe.[22] As Judge McAllister passed through Georgia in 1853 he was very nearly elected to the United States Senate by its legislature.[23]

To his misfortune Judge McAllister had left his capital in the hands of his son Hall, who proved to be an impetuous and unsuccessful plunger. Ward writes: "Grand speculations to double my father's fortune very soon made inroads in it, and the dear old gentleman to save a remnant returned to this country." The "dear old gentleman" also returned with a plan he confided to Ward:

> As he expressed himself to me, "California must have a Circuit Judge of the United States. I will get our Democratic Congress to pass a bill to this effect, and will myself return to California as its United States Circuit Judge. I do not care to return to the practice of law when I reach San Francisco, where, I expect to find that, like the 'fruit of the Dead Sea,' my little competency will turn into ashes at the touch. Being on the Bench, I shall at least have a support. . ."[24]

The only impediment lay in the fact that Ward had arranged to be appointed secretary of legation to James Buchanan, an old friend of his father, who was going to England as United States minister. Ward was no match for his father:

> He came to me and stated the case as follows: "My boy," he said, "the President says he cannot give two appointments to one family. If you go to England as Buchanan's Secretary, President Pierce cannot make me Circuit Judge of California." "Enough said," I replied, "I yield with pleasure."[25]

Judge McAllister held the July 1855 term pursuant to statute and sat in California into the year 1861. By January 1862 his health had declined to the point that the attorney general was thereafter obliged to give him a six-month leave of absence.[26] On January 12, 1863 Judge McAllister wrote from New York to President Abraham Lincoln, resigning his commission, and two years later he died in San Francisco.[27] By the Act of March 3, 1863, eight years and a day after Judge McAllister's court's creation, Congress provided that "the said circuit court is hereby abolished," and established a Tenth Circuit to include California and a tenth Supreme Court justice for that circuit who would be Mr. Justice Stephen J. Field.[28]

Judge McAllister's epitaph, and his court's principal legacy, is a rarely seen volume of decisions published in New York in 1859 by his son and deputy clerk, Cutler: *Reports of Cases Argued and Determined in the Circuit Court of the United States for the Districts of California*. Indeed, his last major opinion, in January 1861, on the merits of the New Almaden Mine case, never got beyond the steam presses of San Francisco; its only mention in West's Federal Cases (No. 14,747) is its caption, *United States v. Andres Castillero*, and the statement: "Nowhere reported; opinion not now accessible." Ironically, that case marked the last appearance in the courts of the United States of Judah P. Benjamin, who represented the prevailing Castillero interests before the judge whose office he had opposed in the Senate five years before.

All this was in the future on June 21, 1856. One substantial change in the structure and duties of the court had occurred by an amendment to the original legislation, enacted on April 30, 1856.[29] The terms of the court were changed from one to four, two in San Francisco in January and July, and two in Los Angeles in March and September. Section 2 of the act provided that the circuit court should be composed of the circuit judge and the district judge of the district in which the court was held, either to be a quorum, and each to be vested with all the power and jurisdiction vested in the several circuit courts of the United States and their judges. So it was that Judge Ogden Hoffman joined Judge McAllister on the bench of the circuit court just two weeks before the events leading to its greatest challenge were set in motion.

Overleaf: Title page of McAllister's Reports.

REPORTS

OF

CASES ARGUED AND DETERMINED

IN THE

CIRCUIT COURT OF THE UNITED STATES

FOR THE

DISTRICTS OF CALIFORNIA.

CUTLER McALLISTER,

REPORTER.

VOLUME I.

NEW YORK:
JOHN S. VOORHIES, LAW BOOKSELLER AND PUBLISHER,
20 NASSAU STREET.
1859.

II

THE RISING

There had been Committees of Vigilance in San Francisco before, a few rudimentary ones before California's statehood and, more recently, a large and well-organized committee which had been active from June to September 1851, hanging or banishing notorious hoodlums. The 1856 committee was different. In the trappings of ad hoc enforcers of law and order like the 1851 committee, the members of the 1856 committee were in fact conservative revolutionaries. Those in control of its executive committee, as well as the committee's substantial financial supporters, were, in the words of its leader, "northern and western men, chiefly representing the mercantile, manufacturing and vested interests," who had been, and sought to resume their status as, the city's elite.[30] As a group these men, whose ascendancy had been unchallenged at the time of the 1851 committee, had since found themselves ravaged by economic slumps in 1854 and 1855, ever prey to lightning-fast changes in supply and demand beyond their control, and threatened by the upward mobility of more recent arrivals. By 1856 they were being increasingly displaced from local political power by their self-interested pursuit of business in the face of the growing entrenchment of David C. Broderick's Tammany-type political machine, which was increasingly threatening their existence by its fiscal mismanagement, high taxation, and soaring municipal indebtedness. Acts of violence of the supporters of this political machine and those it protected and a perceived stultification of law enforcement by the alliance between the local courts and the machine were the catalysts for a rising which displaced the municipal authorities by force of arms, held the state government at bay and maintained an uneasy co-existence with the local representatives of the government of the United States. The criminal "justice" dispensed by the 1856 committee was a means to a political, economic and social end.[31]

It started on the evening of November 17, 1855, when, on Clay Street, William H. Richardson, the United States marshal for the northern district of California, was shot to death at close range by Charles Cora, a gambler and a pimp. The occasion did not involve the marshal's official business: Richardson, who was drunk at the time, fancied that Cora had insulted him, and Cora claimed that he had fired only to save his own life.[32] Despite the strong public prejudice against Cora and the participation in his prosecution by the United States district attorney, Samuel W. Inge, the jury disagreed.[33] In May 1856 Cora was still in jail, awaiting a retrial.

On the afternoon of May 14, 1856, James King of William, a twice-failed banker and now the crusading editor of the *Daily Evening Bulletin*, was shot down from across Montgomery Street by James P. Casey, a small-time politician and county supervisor. The immediate cause of the shooting was a recent series of articles in the *Bulletin* voicing King's objections to the candidacy for a position at the customs house of John W. Bagley; the ground taken for Bagley's unsuitability was his pending indictment for attempting to murder Casey, whom King in turn described as a ballet box stuffer of Broderick's who had served time at Sing Sing before coming west.[34]

John D. Gordan, III

San Francisco in 1856. Taken near the intersection of Harrison and First streets on the since leveled Rincon Hill, this view looks north toward the harbor and downtown area. In 1856 future Civil War

Authorized By No Law

general William T. Sherman lived in the house on the lower right. (Courtesy California Historical Society, San Francisco.)

King, who had a considerable popular following, did not die immediately, although he would on May 20. Casey, for his own protection, was hustled off to jail by Sheriff Scannell's men, who had evidently been forewarned that King was to be shot. On the evening of the shooting, a large crowd of angry citizens had assembled in front of the jail.[35]

By 7:00 P.M., just a few hours after King had been shot, members of the 1851 committee approached William Tell Coleman, a merchant who had been its second-in-command, to reestablish the committee. After perfunctory resistance, Coleman agreed on condition that he be given absolute authority, and a notice issued in the name of the 1851 committee that its members were to meet the next morning.[36] During the next twenty-four hours, fifteen hundred men flocked to join the committee.[37] On May 16 the Committee of Vigilance of San Francisco was "reorganized" with Coleman at its head. By May 17 five thousand members — some ten percent of the total population of San Francisco — filled the committee's ranks, its constitution had been adopted, and the building on Sacramento Street which would become Fort Gunnybags had been acquired.[38]

The committee's opponents, those who favored "law and order" — or, in the committee's view, the status quo of violence and political corruption — were not slow to react. On May 16 the sheriff summoned a posse to mount guard at the jail, made up primarily of "lawyers or persons in some way friendly to those in jail." One of the posse, Hall McAllister, was sent by its members to offer its command to William T. Sherman, a San Francisco banker who, on May 12, had accepted from Governor J. Neely Johnson what he had supposed would be a ceremonial position as major-general commanding the Second Division of the California militia. Although the military forces he commanded existed only on paper, General Sherman was quick to decline captaincy of a civilian posse and instead waited on Governor Johnson, who arrived the same afternoon from Sacramento. That evening General Sherman joined the governor in meetings with William T. Coleman and other members of the executive committee of the Committee of Vigilance.[39]

The accounts of what occurred at these meetings — indeed how many they were and where — are various. Coleman's later version describes an early, apparently private meeting between Governor Johnson and Coleman at which the governor promised to support the committee. This was followed, if it in fact occurred, by two meetings later that night, with General Sherman in attendance, at which the governor urged the committee not to take the law into its own hands and which ended with an agreement that the committee might post ten of its own men as guards in the jail holding Casey and Cora, in return for its undertaking to take no steps against the jail without withdrawing those men and giving notice of doing so. The committee's representatives were admitted to the jail in the early hours of Saturday, May 17.[40]

The stand-off lasted one day. Sunday morning, May 18, the committee sent Governor Johnson a one-sentence notice: "We beg to advise you that we have withdrawn our guard from the county jail." Then, in General Sherman's words: "...masses of people began to move toward the jail, crowning all the houses and hills, soon followed by the Committee in full organization — 2500 men armed with muskets, rifles, a field piece, besides as many more arm in arm, silent, orderly and

William Tell Coleman. Second in command of the 1851 Vigilance Committee, Coleman headed the 1856 committee. (Courtesy The Bancroft Library.)

quiet..."[41] The sheriff capitulated. Coleman brought out Casey first; Cora followed. Both were taken by carriage to Fort Gunnybags.[42]

A day in secret session was followed by the trial, starting at noon on May 20, of Charles Cora before the executive committee. Lawyers, viewed by the committee not only as their opponents but also as the source of many of the problems in the city, were not admitted. At 6:00 P.M. Cora was convicted. While Cora's trial was under way, James King of William died of his wound. Casey's trial for his murder began at 8:00 P.M. and quickly resulted in his conviction. Both were sentenced to be hanged. The larger, representative board of delegates of the Vigilance Committee promptly and unanimously confirmed the actions of the executive committee.[43]

On May 22 at 1:20 P.M., as King's funeral cortege began to move to the cemetery amid the tolling of churchbells, Casey and Cora were hanged from beams run out from the roof of Fort Gunnybags above the second floor rooms of the executive committee, with armed detachments of the Vigilance Committee drawn up in military array and a large crowd looking on. Just before he dropped the trap the committee's ad hoc hangman, Sterling Hopkins, an old foe of Casey's, quietly expressed to Casey his personal satisfaction in having the opportunity to perform this task.[44]

After the executions of Casey and Cora, the committee began rounding up some thirty persons deemed, in Coleman's words, "notorious ballot-box stuffers and other desperate characters," to be transported abroad and not to return under penalty of death. Among these adherents to or sympathizers with the Broderick machine were Charles P. Duane, until recently the chief engineer of the San Francisco Fire Department, and Martin Gallagher, employed by the U.S. government as a night watchman. At two o'clock on the morning of June 5, Duane, Gallagher and four others were placed on the steam tug *Hercules* and carried out to the steamer *Golden Gate* and to the barque *Yankee*, whose destinations were, respectively, Panama and Hawaii.

During this period those who opposed the Vigilance Committee — a group of lawyers, Southerners and municipal politicians confederated as the "Law and Order party," Governor J. Neely Johnson, his major general, William T. Sherman, and Associate Justice David S. Terry of the California Supreme Court, already well known for the violence which would dog his future — began a series of unsuccessful efforts to overcome their impotence by involving the federal authorities on the scene. By the end of May, Johnson, Sherman and Justice Terry had developed the stratagem that Terry would issue a writ of habeas corpus for one Billy Mulligan, a Broderick adherent who had been taken in the same roundup with Duane and Gallagher, in the hope that, once the writ was defied by the Vigilance Committee, the state militia could be called up by Governor Johnson and armed with weapons supplied to the state government by local federal commanders.[45]

On May 30 Justice Terry went to San Francisco to issue the writ for Mulligan.[46] The same day Governor Johnson and General Sherman called on Major General John E. Wool, commanding the Department of the Pacific, at Benicia and on Commodore David G. Farragut, commanding the naval forces and installation at Mare Island. Farragut declined to intervene and was for the moment supported by Commander E.B. Boutwell of the U.S.S. *John Adams*, in transit from Hawaii.[47] General Wool, on the other hand, evidently intimated and at a meeting the following day, according to Sherman and Johnson, promised that although only the president had legal authority to do so, the general would honor a request by the governor to supply arms to the state militia once it was called out by the governor to repress the committee.[48] On May 31 Justice Terry issued the writ, and the Vigilance Committee, having stalled the deputy sheriff long enough to smuggle Mulligan out of Fort Gunnybags, invited a search of the empty premises.[49] Treating this as a defiance of the process of the court, by proclamation of June 3 Governor Johnson called out the state militia, directing it to report to General Sherman, and demanded that the Vigilance Committee disband.[50] The following day the governor transmitted to General Wool a

The execution of Casey and Cora. The Vigilance Committee hanged the two accused murderers as one of its first acts. (Courtesy The Bancroft Library.)

written request for such arms as General Sherman might require, or the governor might order, to suppress the committee, but on June 5 General Wool refused, claiming that he lacked the necessary order of the president.[51] On June 6 General Sherman sent a polite letter to General Wool expressing disbelief that Wool had meant to refuse the arms Sherman thought he had promised on May 31.[52] On June 7 Governor Johnson sent his own strongly-worded letter which concluded with a request for "3000 stand of muskets or rifles, 50 rounds of ammunition, 2 mortars, 300 shells, and 2 guns of large calibre as you have, with their ammunition and appliances."[53]

In the meantime General Sherman had enlisted a group of moderate and respected men not members of the Vigilance Committee, led by J.B. Crockett, a future justice of the California Supreme Court, to act as intermediaries between the governor and the committee, which in turn took a very conciliatory stance, offering to obey all court process and to cease all further military displays if the state militia were disbanded. On June 7 Sherman and the intermediaries arrived at Benicia to meet the governor there. Sherman took the opportunity to try to talk General Wool out of his refusal to provide arms, but without avail. The governor then arrived, with Justice Terry and others to whom the committee was particularly opposed, and demanded that the intermediaries who had come with Sherman apply in writing for permission to see him. He and Justice Terry received them rudely, and the governor later had delivered to them a written ultimatum as his reply to the committee.

General Sherman resigned his commission on the spot, and the committee revoked its offer to the governor.[54]

On June 9 the committee published a lengthy proclamation asserting its intention to persist in its purposes "peaceably if we can, forcibly if we must."[55] The same day General Wool replied to Governor Johnson's letter of June 7, stating that after consulting the applicable laws and regulations he had concluded that only the president had the power to furnish arms to quell an insurrection.[56]

On June 19 Governor Johnson wrote directly to President Franklin Pierce, complaining of General Wool's conduct and asking that he be ordered to furnish the arms requested.[57] On July 19 Secretary of State William Marcy responded that the president declined to do so and enclosed a copy of a lengthy opinion letter from Attorney General Caleb Cushing to the president, advising that legal prerequisites for any intervention by the president had not been satisfied.[58] Because of the distances involved, it is doubtful that Governor Johnson knew the president's position before mid-August.

III

JUNE 21, 1856

General Wool's letter of June 9 to the governor, even as it refused to provide arms to repress an insurrection, did express a willingness to provide to the California authorities from the arsenal at Benicia the annual quota of weapons to which they were entitled. In consequence, even as the governor wrote in complaint to the president, the "next movement" of Major General Volney E. Howard, Sherman's replacement, was, as Commodore Farragut later reported to the secretary of the navy, "to procure a few stand of arms from General Wool, which were due the State by annual distribution."[59] General Howard detailed three members of the state militia, James Reuben Molony, John G. Phillips and James McNabb, to Benicia to collect the arms — which consisted of 113 muskets, one sabre and two bullet molds — and to bring them to him in San Francisco. Late on June 20 they were loaded from the government wharf there onto the schooner *Julia*, chartered by Molony for the purpose. The *Julia* put out into San Pablo Bay and, meeting a headwind, anchored for the night near San Pablo Point, fifteen miles from San Francisco and three miles from the Contra Costa shore.[60]

The Vigilance Committee learned of General Howard's plans. Its grand marshal, Charles Doane, sent for John L. Durkee, until recently a San Francisco policeman, and directed him to pick out a dozen men for "special duty." This accomplished, Doane told Durkee, as the latter later recalled, that "there was a sloop at the foot of the street and... for me and the men to take it and cruise between here and Benicia, to intercept a vessel, supposed to have arms on her belonging to the law and order party. We cruised round and overhauled some vessels." About two hours after midnight on June 21 Durkee "saw a vessel lying under Pablo Point and boarded her, and found a

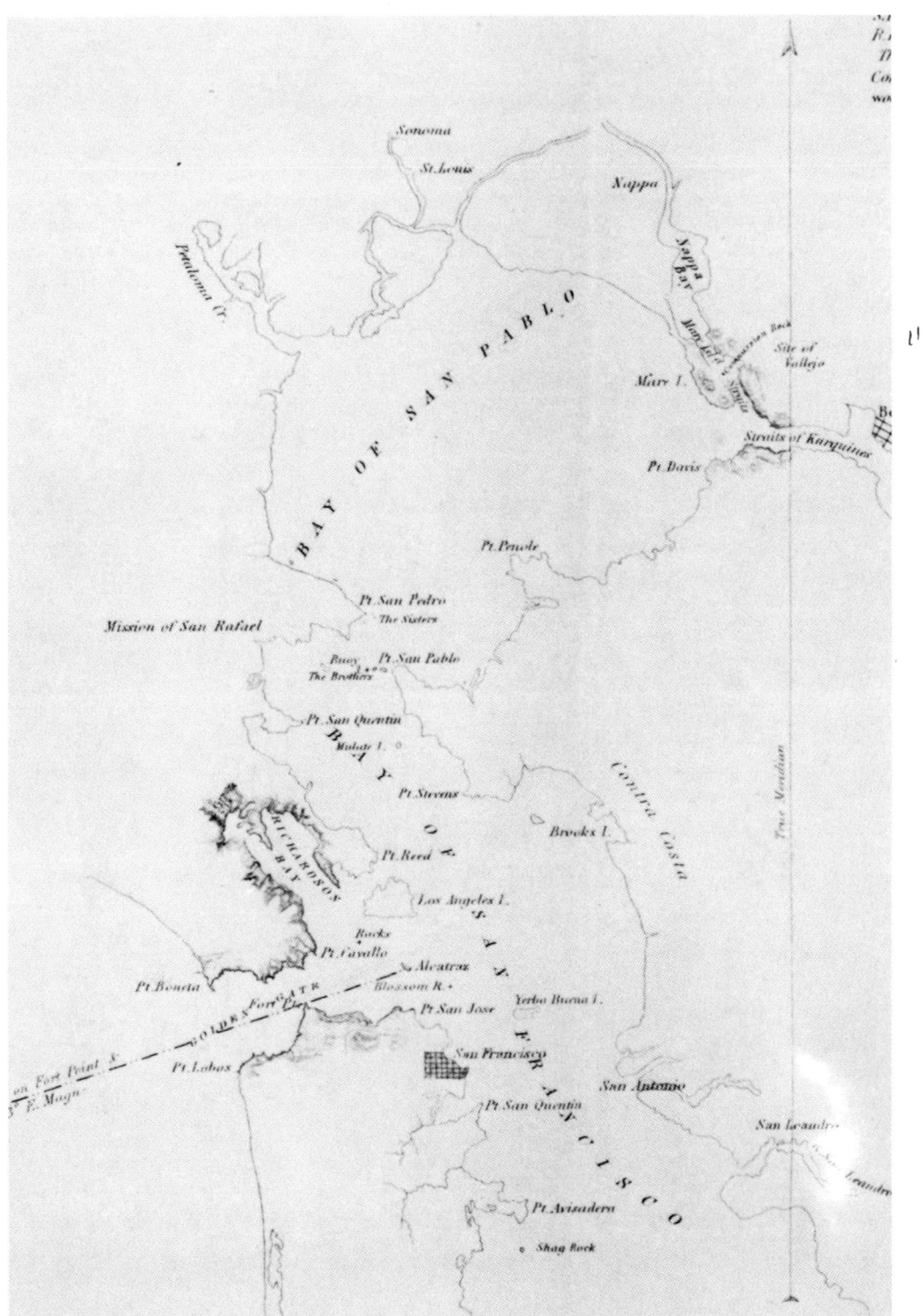

San Pablo Bay. Point San Pablo, where the Julia *was boarded, is on the east side of the entrance to San Pablo Bay from San Francisco Bay.*

John D. Gordan, III

The boarding of the Julia by the Vigilance Committee. This view of the boarding appeared in Frank Leslie's Illustrated Newspaper *on August 9, 1856.*

man named Phillips, Jim McNabb, and Rube Molony, who had charge of these arms. When we got alongside they were all asleep and before they knew it we were in the companion-way and transferring the guns and sabres to our vessel. They made no resistance, and we brought them with us to San Francisco. After getting down, I sent one of the men to the [committee] rooms to report, and was ordered to let the three men go which we did." The muskets were delivered to the executive committee at Fort Gunnybags.[61]

Upon his release about eight o'clock in the morning, Phillips lost no time in appearing before George Penniston Johnston, commissioner of the United States circuit court, to swear out a complaint against Durkee and three other individuals named only as "Rand," "Andrews" and "Hutton." The charge against the four was that:

> ... in the Bay of San Pablo, where the sea ebbs and flows, [they] did commit the crime of robbery in and upon a vessel to wit the "Julia" a schooner so called, and upon the lading thereof - and did feloniously and piratically overhaul, board and rob the said vessel of a large quantity of muskets the property of the State of California - and with force and arms did commit other injuries to and on board of the said vessel - contrary to the acts of congress in such case made and provided and against the peace and dignity of the United States.

The commissioner immediately issued a warrant of arrest for the defendants named in the complaint.[62]

By the early afternoon of June 21 the executive committee had changed its mind about leaving Molony and Phillips at liberty; Sherman suggests in a contemporaneous letter that the cause was the complaint against Durkee and the others before the United States commissioner.[63] About two in the afternoon, Sterling Hopkins, Casey's executioner, and two other committee policemen, D.W. Barry and Horace Russell, arrived at the office of R.P. Ashe, an officer in the state militia and also U.S. naval agent in San Francisco, on the second floor of the building housing Palmer, Cook & Co. on Washington Street. Hopkins and Russell went upstairs and found Molony in the company of Ashe, Justice Terry, McNabb and two or three other Law and Order party adherents. Only Hopkins was admitted, and the door was then locked behind him. After Hopkins told Molony he had a warrant from the Vigilance Committee for his arrest and seized him, Justice Terry drew a knife and someone else put a pistol to Hopkins' head. Ashe pushed Hopkins out the door, saying: "Tell your Committee that they can't arrest anybody in my office."

As Hopkins hurried on a borrowed horse to Fort Gunnybags for reinforcements, Ashe raced to the nearby county treasurer's office to get himself a shotgun and, on his return, urged the others to take refuge in the armory of the San Francisco Blues, his company in the state militia, located a short distance away at Jackson and Dupont streets. They dashed out into the street with Ashe and Justice Terry bringing up the rear, shotguns at the ready.

Hopkins came riding back, dismounted and, with Russell, James S. Bovee, and

UNITED STATES OF AMERICA,

~~Northern~~ District of California, ss:

The President of the United States of America,

To the Marshal of the United States for the Northern District of California, and to his deputies, or any or either of them, GREETING:

Whereas, complaint on oath hath been made to me, charging that *Hutton, J. L. Durkee, Chas. E. Rand, & Andrews* on or about the *21st* day of *June* in the year of our Lord one thousand eight hundred and fifty- *six* on the high seas and within the admiralty and maritime jurisdiction of the United States, to wit: at the District aforesaid, and within the jurisdiction of the honorable the *Circuit* ~~District~~ Court of the ~~Northern~~ District of California, *did commit the crime of robbery in and upon a vessel to wit: the "Julia" a schooner so called, & upon the lading thereof, and did feloniously and piratically overhaul, board, and rob the said vessel of a large quantity of muskets the property of the State of Cal.*

Now, therefore, you are hereby commanded, in the name of the President of the United States of America, to apprehend the said *Hutton, J. L. Durkee, Chas E Rand, & Andrews* and bring *their* bod*ies* forthwith before me, Commissioner appointed by the *Circuit* ~~District~~ Court of the United States for the ~~Northern~~ District of California, at my office, ~~at~~ *forthwith* that *they* may then and there be dealt with according to law for the said offence.

GIVEN under my hand and seal, this *21st* day of *June* in the year of our Lord one thousand eight hundred and *fifty six* and of our Independence the ~~seventy~~ *eightieth*. —

Geo. Pen. Johnstone
U. S. Commissioner for the ~~Northern~~ District of California.

Arrest warrant for John L. Durkee, Charles E. Rand, and others for their seizure of muskets from the Julia. This order was issued by George Penniston Johnston, commissioner of the United States Circuit Court for the Districts of California. (Courtesy National Archives - San Francisco Branch.)

Justice Terry stabbing Sterling Hopkins. (Courtesy The Bancroft Library.)

two other committee policemen, gave chase to Ashe's group, which was now running up Kearny Street. At the corner of Kearny and Jackson, Justice Terry and Ashe wheeled around and leveled their shotguns. Hopkins, who was unarmed, grappled with Justice Terry for his shotgun. Bovee grabbed Ashe's shotgun and stuck his pistol against Ashe's ear; Ashe let the shotgun go. As Russell removed Ashe's pistol from its holster, he was jostled and his own pistol discharged into the coat of one of the other committee officers. At that moment, Justice Terry let go of his shotgun, drew his Bowie knife and plunged it deep into Hopkins' neck, slicing into his larynx and carotid artery. Hopkins staggered off down the street, bleeding heavily. Ashe and Justice Terry then raced to the armory a block away where the rest of their party had already taken refuge.[64]

The committee reacted swiftly. Its full military force was immediately summoned by the alarm bell on the roof of Fort Gunnybags and drawn up, together with two artillery pieces, in front of the armory and in the surrounding streets. Grand Marshal Doane demanded the armory's immediate surrender — "open the doors or I will blow up the building." Ashe, the senior officer present, sent out a note agreeing to surrender "if the executive committee will give us protection from violence." The

Justice Terry and other prisoners being escorted to Vigilance Committee headquarters. This procession followed the surrender of Justice Terry and others at the armory of the San Francisco Blues, a militia company. (Courtesy The Bancroft Library.)

executive committee responded that it would, provided Justice Terry, Molony, Phillips and the contents of the armory were immediately handed over. Noting that Phillips was not there, Ashe accepted the terms and opened the doors.[65]

The prisoners were driven to Fort Gunnybags surrounded by a large force of armed men. At the same time, other Vigilance Committee forces were quickly detailed to the remaining Law and Order party strongpoints in the city, whose occupants surrendered themselves and their arms.[66] The power of the Vigilance Committee over the state and local governments was now unchallenged, but the collision with federal authority so carefully avoided by the executive committee had now occurred.

The reverberations of the events of June 21 continued in pretrial proceedings in two courts, one of law and one extralegal. The executive committee, although appalled at the prospect of having to hang Justice Terry in the event of Hopkins' death, resolved that his trial would begin before them on June 22; in the end it did not start until June 27.[67] In the meantime both appeals and threats, for and from Terry, cascaded upon the committee. On June 21 Major General Howard issued a bombastic demand that Justice Terry be released to "the custody of the officers of the law alone," which the committee ignored.[68] On June 24 Terry himself wrote to the committee, asking for a trial before "a legal tribunal in this city" with a jury satisfactory to the committee and offering to resign from the bench and leave the state if Hopkins should die, even if acquitted. This appeal, too, was disregarded.[69]

Much more troublesome to the committee were the activities of Commander Boutwell of the *John Adams*, which had dropped down from Mare Island for repairs to its sails and lay just off the city at the foot of Sacramento Street. Boutwell had intervened early and successfully on behalf of Ashe, the Navy's local agent, who had been taken with Justice Terry and Molony at the armory.[70] On June 27 Governor Johnson addressed a strongly-worded plea to Boutwell,[71] followed the next day by this one from Terry himself:

> Sir: I desire to inform you that I am a native born citizen of the United States, and one of the justices of the supreme court of the State of California, and that, on the 21st day of June instant, I was seized with force and violence by an armed body of men styling themselves the "Vigilance Committee," and was conveyed by them to a *fort* which they had erected and formidably entrenched with cannon in the heart of the city of San Francisco; and that, since that time, I have been held a prisoner in close custody, and guarded day and night by large bodies of armed men with muskets and bayonets, by order of the said committee. I desire further to inform you that the said committee is a powerful organization of men, acting in open and armed rebellion against the lawful authorities of this State; that they have resisted by force the execution of the writ of *habeas corpus*, and have publicly declared, through their organs, that *their will* was the *supreme law* of the State.
>
> The government of the State has already made ineffectual efforts to quell this rebellion, and the traitors, emboldened by *success*, have already *hung two men* and banished a great many others, and some of their members now openly threaten to seize the *forts* and *arsenals* of the United States as well as the ships of war in port, and secede from the federal Union.
>
> During my imprisonment I have suffered the indignity of being *handcuffed* by these rebels, my friends are denied all access to me, and all kinds of terrorism are resorted to to compel me to resign my office.
>
> I desire further to inform you, that said committee is now engaged in trying me as a criminal for attempting resistance to their authority, and also for an assault with intent to kill one of their members, whilst I acted solely in defence of my own life against their assaults on the public streets, and that I am in hourly danger of suffering an *ignominious death* at the hands of these traitors and assassins.
>
> In this emergency I invoke the protection of the *flag of my country*.
>
> I call on you promptly to interfere, with all the powers at your disposal, to protect my life from the impending peril...[72]

On June 28 Boutwell responded with a "request" to the executive committee that they treat Terry "as a prisoner of war, and place him aboard my ship,"[73] but his answer to the governor on June 29 reflected the impotence of his position, despite the firepower of his warship:

> I could destroy the city of San Francisco with the guns of the John Adams, but in the ruin, friends as well as others would suffer.
>
> If I could persuade the committee to set Judge Terry at liberty, I should be most happy to do so. If I demand his release, and they fail to give him up, I

must either batter the town down or render myself ridiculous in the eyes of the world, and incur the displeasure of my government, neither of which is consonant with my present feelings.[74]

The committee, however, decided to deflect Boutwell by going over his head to Commodore Farragut. On June 29 the secretary of the executive committee, under his customary soubriquet "33, Secretary," forwarded Boutwell's letter to Farragut.[75] On July 1, Farragut responded, nominally supporting Boutwell, but promising to "pour oil on the troubled waters."[76] The same day, he addressed a stiff letter to Boutwell, anticipating much of what Attorney General Cushing would say to the president in his letter of July 19 and stating flatly that "I cannot agree that you have any right to interfere in this matter..." without explicit orders from Washington.[77] Boutwell responded with a thinly-veiled suggestion that Farragut was a hypocrite and the assertion that he was not Boutwell's commanding officer anyway.[78] Farragut's reply was astoundingly mild, but firm. While acknowledging that he was not Boutwell's commanding officer and that "I should not have interfered with you, but for cause," Farragut stated that "you must be aware that you can not be beyond my control so long as you are within these waters." Farragut continued that, as the superior officer present, he would "act according to the best judgment for the general good." He assured Boutwell that the latter's views would be communicated to Washington, where "[y]our course may be more approved than mine."[79] He did, however, authorize Boutwell to "receive on board Judge D.S. Terry, for his personal safety, should any arrangement be made to accomplish that end."[80]

At the same moment as the Vigilance Committee was preparing to try Justice Terry, the proceedings initiated before the United States commissioner were moving forward. On June 22 Durkee was arrested by two deputy United States marshals and was held at the marshal's office at Battery and Washington Streets for a preliminary hearing before the commissioner the next morning. Durkee offered no resistance, for, as he later said: "Had I refused to go, the Committee would not have let me go and then the U.S. Government and the Committee would have been at loggerheads. It struck me like a flash that it was best for me to go." Several members of the executive committee visited him there and told him not to be uneasy.[81]

In preparation for the preliminary hearing, a subpoena issued for Molony, Phillips and McNabb to appear as witnesses. The last two named were served, but Molony was at Fort Gunnybags in the hands of the Vigilance Committee, which repeated the same techniques it had used with Justice Terry's writ the month before.[82] According to later testimony[83] of the United States marshal for the northern district of California, James Y. McDuffie:

[O]ne of my Deputies, Mr. Palmer, went to serve the process, he afterwards informed me he was detained at the door and prevented from going in; I don't recollect how long, and that he was afterwards admitted; and I returned the process "not found", not being able to find him.[84]

According to Molony, "I was taken out the back way, into a building in the rear,

Subpoena for James R. Molony and others. Molony, who was on board the Julia when it was seized, was subpoenaed to be a witness in Durkee's committal proceeding. Because he was in the hands of the Vigilance Committee the United States marshal was unsuccessful in serving the document. (Courtesy National Archives - San Francisco Branch.)

which entered on the main fortress...surrounded by an armed force of some twenty men."[85]

At the preliminary hearing on June 23, Durkee was represented by William Duer and J.B. Crockett, the former head of General Sherman's committee of intermediaries. His request for an adjournment for one day was granted. The commissioner committed not only Durkee to the custody of the marshal but also, as material witnesses, Phillips and McNabb, evidently out of concern that the Vigilance Committee might make them as unavailable as Molony.[86] To assure his ability to retain them in custody, Marshal McDuffie arranged to keep the latter two aboard a U.S. revenue cutter.[87]

The energetic activities of McDuffie, who had been a frequent target of James King of William, did not pass unnoticed by the Vigilance Committee. On the evening of June 23 a delegation of the executive committee waited on McDuffie and "cautioned me, that myself and Mr. Johnston would probably get into a worse scrape than Durkee did, if we didn't mind how we interfered with that Committee."[88]

On June 24 there was a further one-day adjournment, and on June 25, according to the commissioner's records, Durkee's counsel "admitted the truth of the statements made in the affidavit on which the warrant issued." The next day there were further proceedings before the commissioner which resulted in his finding that Durkee was guilty as charged and in Durkee's committal to await action by the grand jury.[89] The marshal arranged with Commander Boutwell, who had not yet been reined in by Commodore Farragut, to lodge Durkee aboard the *John Adams*.[90]

The following day Durkee was brought before Judge Hoffman on a writ of habeas corpus.[91] While the papers of the proceedings in the district court are incomplete, it appears that Judge Hoffman released Durkee on $25,000 bail in the first days of July.[92]

On July 5 the executive committee took the opportunity to banish Molony, under penalty of death if he returned, on a steamer bound for Panama.[93] On July 7 Charles E. Rand was arrested on Commissioner Johnston's warrant and immediately admitted to $25,000 bail.[94]

IV

INCIDENT IN THE GULF OF CALIFORNIA

Judge Matthew Hall McAllister played no part in these events, for he was not in San Francisco. His first direct encounter with shock waves of the Vigilance Commitee was on June 23, 1856 in Acapulco, then a coaling station for Pacific Mail line steamers making the run between the west coast of the Isthmus and San Francisco. As the steamship *John L. Stephens* prepared to leave port for the final week-long leg of the journey to San Francisco, Judge McAllister, traveling with his son and deputy clerk of court, Cutler, encountered an exile of the Vigilance Committee who had tricked his way aboard without a ticket.

This stowaway was Charles P. Duane, who had been taken from San Francisco on June 5 on the steam tug *Hercules* and placed aboard the *Golden Gate*. Although the Vigilance Committee had intended that he should be carried to Panama, Duane had managed to escape under cover of darkness when the *Golden Gate* arrived in Acapulco on June 13. He hid for ten days and then, penniless but determined to return to San Francisco despite the Vigilance Committee's threat to hang him if he did, he managed to board the *John L. Stephens* at dawn on June 23 by the ruse at the gangway that his ticket was in his stateroom aboard.

Duane, who walked about openly once on board, found that the judge and Cutler McAllister were not the only people known to him; others included a former treasurer

Authorized By No Law

Deportation of Charles P. Duane from San Francisco by the Vigilance Committee. (Courtesy The Bancroft Library.)

of San Francisco county, Charles Scott, and many of the ship's officers, including her captain, Robert H. Pearson. Although Scott offered to pay Duane's passage, Duane responded that "I would rather get Judge McAllister to pay my fare;" Duane told the judge and Cutler McAllister how he had stood with Hall McAllister in the Law and Order posse which guarded the jail holding Cora and Casey on the night of May 16.

Duane and the judge went to the ship's purser, who declined the judge's offer to pay Duane's passage on instructions from the captain. Judge McAllister also called on Captain Pearson in his cabin and offered to pay Duane's fare, but the captain refused it. The *John L. Stephens* nevertheless departed for San Francisco with Duane on board.

That afternoon Captain Pearson sent for Duane and advised him that, while he was surprised by the reports in the San Francisco papers taken aboard at Acapulco of Duane's treatment by the Vigilance Committee, he was an adherent of the committee and had no wish to bring Duane back to San Francisco. Threatening to hold Duane for the Vigilance Committee if he were aboard on arrival in San Francisco, Captain Pearson said that, if they met the steamer *Sonora* as she headed south towards Acapulco, he would put Duane aboard her. Duane resolutely insisted on being taken back to San Francisco.

The next few days passed uneventfully, Duane eating in the dining room as if he were a regular passenger. However, on the evening of June 26, as Duane would later testify:

The John L. Stephens. *(Courtesy National Maritime Museum - San Francisco.)*

> We met the "Sonora" in the Gulf of California. I saw her myself; called Cutler McAllister's attention to it. . .

The *Sonora* and the *John L. Stephens* stopped, and Captain Pearson went aboard the *Sonora* to talk to her captain. About midnight he sent instructions that Duane was to be brought aboard the *Sonora*. Duane's account continues:

> I then went and asked some ladies I knew to allow me the use of their room. They begged me not to go there. I then went down into the water-closet. The steamer was stopped; peeped out; saw all hands searching. After a while one of the men came and pulled the water-closet door open. He shouted, "Here he is;" "here he is." I got out of the window; drew myself along the promenade deck to where they stowed the cattle. They were wild; stuck their horns into me; got under the life-boat on the promenade deck; remained there about half an hour; finally hoisted the boat up; I jumped out; they rushed for me; about sixty or seventy were looking for me. I had a knife which a passenger lent me. I drew it and said I was ready to defend myself. Some fifty or one hundred rushed to my rescue; came between me and the parties searching for me, and I got through the crowd.
>
> On the promenade deck I met Cutler McAllister, who advised me not to resist, they were determined to take me. The parties in pursuit of me came up again. The first mate was in charge. I drew my knife again, determined to defend myself. The first mate said, "Charley, it isn't my wish, but the captain says I must do it." I said the captain had no authority to seize me and put me

off the steamer; that he, the mate, was hired to do other work than that; that if he touched me I certainly would kill him. I backed up so that they couldn't get behind me. The passengers appeared to arm themselves, and said they must not interfere with me; told me not to be afraid, they would defend me. I had to plead very hard to stop them; told them I didn't wish a mutiny on board on my account; saw the mate cocking his pistol; said, shoot away, you can't intimidate me. The passengers said, put up your pistol. I think he put it up.

I remained in this position for some 15 or 20 minutes. They couldn't get near me. I had made up my mind not to go living; allowed no one to get nearer to me than they were —about eight feet—neither as a friend nor in any other way.

Judge McAllister came through the crowd. He said: Duane, put your knife away; don't cut anybody, or the captain will hang you at the yard-arm, as he has done so before. Said he, I don't advise you to go, but don't cut anybody. I knew he was a friend. I took his advise; put my knife away, and cried like a child. I couldn't help it.

They came and dragged me away to the side of the ship. There was a great confusion on board; passengers cried, "Shame!" "shame!" Judge McAllister said to the mate, "You shall be held responsible for this high-handed measure on the high seas." The passengers gathered around Judge McAllister, and his pleading prevented them from rescuing me. They took me down the ladder of the Stephens, put me in a small boat, and rowed to the Sonora...

Duane's protests were, for the time being, in vain; the *Sonora* carried him back to Acapulco. Judge McAllister would never sit in judgment of the conduct of the officers of the *John L. Stephens*, but his opinion, three years later, in an action brought by Martin Gallagher, one of Duane's fellow passengers on the *Hercules* on June 5, shows the judge's lack of sympathy with the extra-legal conduct of the Vigilance Committee:

That sentence [of deportation from California] is ascertained to have been issued by a body of men authorized by no law, and who substituted their private judgments for the action of those judicial tribunals to which the constitution and laws of their country had confided solely the distribution of justice. With the motives of those who acted thus, this court has nothing to do. With their acts, so far as they bear upon this case, it is its duty to deal. It is, therefore, constrained to attribute to those acts, and to the conduct of the respondent so far as it is connected with them, the character which the law annexes to them and to it.[95]

The *John L. Stephens* continued to San Francisco. She must have arrived on June 30, landing the judge and his clerk just a week before they would open the July 1856 term of the circuit court.[96] On her return trip to Panama, which began on July 5, the *John L. Stephens* would carry, as an unwilling first-class passenger and guest of the Vigilance Committee, James Reuben Molony.

John D. Gordan, III

Justice David S. Terry. (Courtesy California State Library.)

V

THE TRIAL OF JUSTICE TERRY

Justice Terry's trial before the executive committee began on June 27, while Judge McAllister was on the high seas off Baja California. The charges naturally led off with his stabbing of Hopkins: the first was "resisting, by violence, the officers of the Committee of Vigilance, while in the discharge of their duty" and the second "assault, with a deadly weapon, with intent to kill Sterling A. Hopkins, a police officer of the Committee of Vigilance..."[97] In addition, however, the justice was charged with "breaches of the peace and attacks on citizens, when in discharge of their duties," as follows:

3. In 1853, an attack on Mr. Evans, a citizen of Stockton.

4. With an attack on Mr. Roadhouse, a citizen of Stockton, while in the Court House.

5. An attack on Mr. King, a citizen of Stockton, at the Charter election.

6. In 1853, resistance of a writ of Habeas Corpus, by which William Roach escaped from the custody of the law, and the infant heirs of the Sanchez family were defrauded of their rights.

7. In 1853, an attack on J.H. Purdy, in the city of San Francisco.[98]

In the prosecution's case the committee policemen who participated and other eyewitnesses testified to the pursuit of Ashe's party and the struggle with Ashe and Terry for their weapons.[99] By July 17 Hopkins was sufficiently recovered to add his own deposition to a trial record which already contained medical testimony about the gravity of his wound and the emergency surgery to tie his severed artery a few moments before death would have ensued.[100] With the exception of Bovee, the witnesses acknowledged that Terry had merely wrestled with Hopkins to retain his gun and had not drawn his knife until Russell's pistol had gone off.

No evidence was offered on the fifth and sixth charges, and with respect to the assault on Roadhouse, the proof was a copy of Terry's indictment on that charge in the district court for San Joaquin county in 1851, on which were endorsed the jury's guilty verdict and Terry's sentence — a fine of one dollar.[101] However, one L. Villinger was added to the program to testify to Terry's attempt to pistolwhip him a few years before in Stockton because of Villinger's inadequate repair of Terry's watch,[102] and Messrs. Evans and Purdy, the victims identified in the third and seventh counts, did testify.

Evans explained that he and Terry had had a falling out when Evans opposed Terry's unsuccessful candidacy for mayor of Stockton in 1850. On Christmas Eve, 1850, according to Evans, he had encountered a porter employed at the store he ran seriously beaten and had told him to go home. Suddenly, Evans was struck on the head from behind with a pistol wielded by Terry and then beaten into unconsciousness with pistols and clubs by R.P. Ashe, D.W. Perley, Terry's law partner, and Terry

Fort Gunnybags. Deriving its name from its principal fortification, this building at the corner of Sacramento and Front streets was the site of the trial of Justice Terry. (Courtesy California State Library.)

himself, who repeatedly urged, "Kill the damned son of a bitch." Evans learned afterwards that it was the same group that had also beaten his porter and testified that at the time, Terry's "reputation was that of a quarrelsome, ugly, fighting man, whose pistol was out on all occasions; and was in the habit of drawing his knife upon people upon such occasions as I supposed there was a chance to get in a row."[103]

J.H. Purdy, a deputy sheriff of San Francisco county, testified that in September 1853, after publishing in his newspaper without identifying its author a letter from Stockton critical of Terry, he had received a visit from Terry and Perley. When Purdy refused Terry's demand for the name of his correspondent, Terry struck a blow at Purdy's head with a cane he was carrying. Purdy blocked the blow and wrested the cane from Terry, who then threatened to kill him and drew his knife. Afterwards Purdy found he was bleeding from a scalp wound but did not know how it was inflicted.[104]

Here the prosecution rested, and Justice Terry, denied legal counsel in accordance with committee practice, opened his defense. On trial for his life as the prisoner of an extralegal organization he had actively opposed and one of whose members he had critically wounded, Justice Terry's performance proved that, whatever his faults, he was an effective trial lawyer and a brave man. His opening statement to the executive committee began:

> You doubtless feel that you are engaged in a praiseworthy undertaking. This question I will not attempt to discuss; for, whilst I cannot reconcile your acts with my ideas of right and justice, candor forces me to confess that the

evils you arose to repress were glaring and palpable, and the end you seek to attain is a noble one. The question on which we differ is, as to whether the end justifies the means by which you have sought its accomplishment...

Justice Terry then went on to assure the committee that although he opposed it he had no sympathy with the ballot box stuffers and others of that ilk against whom the committee had taken action.[105]

He further explained that on the afternoon of June 21, before Hopkins' first attempt to arrest Molony:

...General Howard and myself had a conversation on the state of affairs, and the utter hopelessness of resisting the Vigilance Committee without money or arms, which the State was unable to procure. In that conversation it was agreed that I should proceed to Sacramento, and endeavor, by proper representations, to procure the order of the Governor directing Gen. Howard to defer all further efforts till a reply was received to the dispatches forwarded to Washington by the last steamer.

* * * *

It may be proper here to state that my position in the matter was not altogether voluntarily assumed. I was urgently requested by gentlemen of undoubted character and standing to take a prominent position, for the reason, as they stated, that it would be useful in keeping the organization alive under the very unfavorable aspect of the contest. At the time I took the first steps I had full assurance that the Governor would be backed with all the munitions of the General Government. In this aspect of affairs, I was confident the struggle would be brought to a speedy and bloodless termination.

* * * *

After the positive refusal of General Wool to furnish to the State any arms, my fidelity to my friends who were in like circumstances with myself, pride, obstinacy, or what you will, prevented my relaxing my efforts as long as a hope remained. After having been frequently misled as to our power to raise funds, finding the effort utterly hopeless, I was about retiring, defeated and dispirited, from the field when I unfortunately became involved in the only collision which occurred during the whole campaign. As I have elsewhere stated, I thought it my duty to resist any infractions of the law attempted in my presence, however little the prospect I may have had of ultimately succeeding. I acted upon this principle. The difference between my position and yours is, that, being a Judicial officer, it is my sworn duty to uphold the law... You, although you may feel assured that you are right, must see that I could not, with any regard to principle or my oath of office, side with you.[106]

Justice Terry also addressed the charges against him. Of the first — resisting the officers of the committee — he said, "This charge is certainly true..." To have done

TRIAL

OF

DAVID S. TERRY

BY THE

COMMITTEE OF VIGILANCE,

SAN FRANCISCO.

SAN FRANCISCO:
R. C. MOORE & CO., PRINTERS, ALTA CALIFORNIA NEWSPAPER OFFICE,
124 SACRAMENTO STREET, NEAR MONTGOMERY.
1856.

Title page of a printed account of the trial of Justice Terry by the Vigilance Committee.

otherwise would have violated his oath as an officer of the law. But Justice Terry denied the second charge, for he said that he believed at the time, and still did so, that Hopkins intended to kill him.[107]

The other charges, Justice Terry said, like the character assassination in the press which he assured the committee he believed they would not be swayed by, were the product of those persons who "having already determined to compass my ruin as far as possible... are anxiously striving to furnish some sort of plausible pretext, and, by reviving and falsifying transactions long past, excite, as far as possible, the mind of the community."[108]

Justice Terry admitted that he had assaulted Purdy, striking him on the head twice with the handle of his knife and being fined three hundred dollars in consequence. He also admitted stabbing Roadhouse in the shoulder at the courthouse in Stockton, but only after Roadhouse, the defendant in an action on trial in which Terry represented the plaintiff, had cursed him and called him a liar.[109]

Terry denied the remaining charges. He admitted striking Evans with a pistol, but said he was assisting R.P. Ashe, then the sheriff in Stockton, when Evans tried to interfere with the arrest of his porter for throwing firecrackers into a wedding party. As to the unproved claim of resisting a writ of habeas corpus, Justice Terry explained that the writ had been issued by a corrupt judge in Monterey in an effort to rescue a prisoner whom Terry's party had arrested by order of a higher court.[110]

The committee allowed Terry to call numerous witnesses, just as it had allowed him to cross examine its own. They substantiated Terry's version of the facts with regard to the charges he denied. So far as the stabbing of Hopkins was concerned, however, they added only a denial that Justice Terry had drawn a knife in Ashe's office and the fact that, before he and Hopkins grappled, Justice Terry had urged the Vigilance Committee policemen to keep back, stating that he was a peace officer.[111] R.P. Ashe, who appeared more than once at the trial, did provide testimony supporting Justice Terry's claim of self-defense and dramatic details of their arrival and surrender at the armory after Hopkins was stabbed:

> ...Terry immediately said, "I wonder who I stabbed," and expressed a hope that the wound would not prove fatal, and that he had acted solely in self-defense; and further said, "Ashe, I saw you reel, and thought they had killed you in the fray." On consultation for surrender I said to him, "I love you more than ever I did human being on earth," and I told him I would die there, with him, selling my life as dearly as possible. His prompt reply was, that he was fully aware of my strong regard for him, bursting into tears; "I hate to surrender to a mob, but I have only acted in self-defense in every aspect of the case, and I will not allow these men (meaning the men of my company) to sacrifice themselves for me; and I know, Ashe, there must be some men on the Committee who are gentlemen, and will not, under the circumstances, see me sacrificed." We then surrendered.[112]

The trial concluded on the evening of July 22, and the next day the executive committee began two days of deliberation on the verdict and sentence. Justice Terry was convicted of two of the charges he had admitted — resisting the officers of the committee and the assault on Purdy. He was also convicted of the second charge — the assault on Hopkins, but without the aggravating factor of intent to kill. The executive committee resolved that Terry should be released and, also, that he should resign his office.[113]

On July 25 the decision of the executive committee was placed before the larger, broad-based board of delegates for confirmation. But after the record of the trial had been read, a motion to approve the verdict and sentence failed to pass. On July 31 the board of delegates voted that the conviction on the second charge include a finding of intent to kill and that the punishment should be exile from the state, with death the penalty for return.[114] Two days earlier, on July 29, on a specially erected scaffold near Fort Gunnybags, with nearly two thousand of the committee's men-at-arms drawn up and hundreds of spectators in the streets and on the rooftops, the committee hanged two murderers, Heatherington and Brace, whose trials had immediately preceded and followed Justice Terry's.

VI

THE WRIT

There is little record of Judge McAllister's response to the state of affairs that greeted him upon his arrival in San Francisco. A.E. Wagstaff, Justice Terry's first biographer, reports that on July 6, Judge McAllister was approached for a writ of habeas corpus for Justice Terry. The writ was refused, the judge stating that he "was unwilling to provoke the animosity of the people."[115]

Assuming Wagstaff's report to be accurate, it appears that during the two succeeding weeks, as Justice Terry's trial continued, Judge McAllister grew bolder. According to a report sent by Commodore Farragut to the secretary of the navy in early August:

> On the 20th day of July I received a note from Judge McAllister, of the Circuit Court of the United States, requesting an interview with me, and, at the same time, a message from Dr. Gwin that he, the Judge, the sub-Treasurer, and the Superintendent of the Branch Mint in San Francisco, would await my arrival until a late hour that night, to consult as to the safety of the funds, papers, etc., of the United States. I could not go down that night, as it was late, calm, and foggy, but went down in the morning at an early hour.
>
> * * * *
>
> Judge McAllister desired to know of me whether, should it become necessary, in his official capacity, to issue a writ of *habeas corpus* for the person of Judge Terry, I would give the United States Marshal the necessary assistance on the water to prevent the abduction of Judge Terry from the harbor of San

Francisco by the associated mobites styling themselves a Vigilance Committee. I told the Judge that, if he could make it clear to me that he had the right to issue the writ, I would give him the assistance; and that, although I was unwilling to move in this matter, I would support the Constitution and laws of the Union to the extent of my power. He informed me that there are very large interests pending before the Supreme Court of the State, and that there are citizens of other States and foreigners who are kept out of their moneys, etc., by the confinement of the Judge, and they had applied to and were anxious for him to have him released. He also showed me the law, with his application of it to the present case; whereupon, being convinced that he had the right to issue the writ, I gave Commander Boutwell orders (a copy herewith forwarded), on the application of the United States Marshal for assistance, under a writ of *habeas corpus*, to render him all in his power to secure the person of Judge Terry, and prevent, if possible, his abduction. I also sent the schooner Fenimore Cooper down to Commander Boutwell, for the purpose of better effecting this end, and she is a very fast sailer. She still lies there.[116]

The singular impetus for Justice Terry's release — the necessity of his presence for the discharge of business by the California Supreme Court — finds confirmation in a passage of a letter William T. Sherman had written on July 2:

> It has now been almost certain that if Hopkins died, Judge Terry would be hung. If Hopkins recovers, then he will be banished. At all events he must be made to resign, but he will not resign, he says. He would rather die than be dishonored. If forced to leave the state, he still remains Judge of the Supreme Court, and as Judge Heydenfelt is away, it virtually breaks up the Supreme Court, that court on which we all depend, we for our city case, on which we believe the judges have passed favorably. Yet this decision is not yet rendered, and therefore as an effect of this outrageous decision, we have to incur the risk and expense of going over the whole case again. Of the judges of the Supreme Court, Murray is an able lawyer, but has all the vices in the calendar. Heydenfelt is an honest, honorable good man, but the extremist "states rights" Calhoun man, he is now abroad. Terry is young, resembles you in appearance, probably taller and heavier, highly honorable and bade fair to make an excellent judge, but he was imprudent in this matter for as judge he ought to have kept aloof on the score that the questions involved might come before him as judge.[117]

Judge McAllister's opinion granting the writ of habeas corpus for Justice Terry[118] is true to the sketchy outline which appears in Commodore Farragut's report of his meeting with the judge.

The applicant for the writ was one des Rochers, a French citizen. He alleged that he was plaintiff in an action against the County of San Francisco for sixteen thousand dollars, which had been argued and submitted at the January 1856 term of the

Supreme Court of California; that the absence of Justice Heydenfeldt from the state reduced the number of justices available to two, the statutory minimum for a quorum, and accordingly that the unlawful imprisonment of Justice Terry since June 21 was preventing both a decision in des Rochers' suit and the holding of the July 1856 term of the California Supreme Court. In conclusion, he asserted that "the persons who hold the said David S. Terry in illegal confinement are about to transfer and convey him beyond the limits of this State and of the United States, illegally and against his will."[119]

In an eight-page opinion largely devoted to a discussion of *United States v. Green*, 3 Mason 482 (C.C.D.R.I. 1824),[120] and the decisions in *United States ex rel. Wheeler v. Williamson*, (E.D. Pa. 1855),[121] referred to as the *Case of Passmore Williamson*, Judge McAllister granted the writ of habeas corpus, finding power to do so, on the authority of those two cases, in Section 14 of the Judiciary Act of 1789. That section conferred jurisdiction "to grant writs of *habeas corpus* for the purpose of an enquiry into the cause of commitment" but restricted that jurisdiction with a concluding proviso that "writs of *habeas corpus*, shall in no case extend to prisoners in gaol, unless where they are in custody, under or by colour of the authority of the United States..." Judge McAllister concluded: "He [Terry] is not in jail, nor in any custody known to the law, but held in restraint against his will, and in direct violation of those laws."

As he certainly knew, Judge McAllister had no jurisdiction to issue the writ. His opinion construed the proviso as prohibiting issuance of the writ only "to any persons in legal custody in jail, unless there under the authority of the United States," but without effect on his power to issue the writ for a person "who is restrained of his liberty by lawless men, who is under no legal restraint..." However, it had long before been settled that Section 14 conferred jurisdiction to issue the writ only for persons held under authority of the United States and not, as Judge McAllister's opinion concluded, for any person restrained of his liberty by anyone, unless in jail under state authority. In *Elkison v. Deliesseline*, 2 Wheeler's Reports of Criminal Cases 56 (C.C.D.S.C. 1823), Justice William Johnson held that:

> The proviso to the fourteenth section of the judiciary act imposes on the petitioner the necessity of maintaining the affirmative of his being *confined under United States' authority*; so that it is not enough to negative his being in custody under state authority, for the consequence is only that he is confined arbitrarily and without authority . . . a case to which our power to issue this writ does not extend.

Id. at 70-71 (emphasis in original).[122] Similarly, of the two precedents upon which Judge McAllister relied, the first had been eroded and the second never entitled to any weight to begin with.

In the first, *United States v. Green*, Justice Story had undeniably issued a writ of habeas corpus in a child custody dispute among private parties, but, as even Judge McAllister conceded, the issue of jurisdiction was never raised. By 1842, while Justice Story was still a sitting justice, Judge Alfred Conkling had delicately questioned the jurisdictional basis for *Green* in his treatise on federal jurisdiction: "It does not appear from the report of the case that the jurisdiction of the court was drawn into question; but it is much to be regretted that the ground upon which it was considered as attaching, was not stated."[123] Two years later, in In Re Barry, 42 Fed. 113 (C.C.S.D.N.Y. 1844), appeal dismissed, Barry v. Mercein, 46 U.S. 103 (1847), Judge Samuel Rossiter Betts refused to follow Green. Noting that, with the exception of Green, "[e]very adjudicated case in the United States courts... has been under writs sued out for relief against an actual arrest of a party under process, or his confinement by claim of authority of the United States," Judge Betts held that "[t]he principles established by the Supreme Court... would seem to militate so strongly against the doctrine involved in the case of United States v. Green as to prevent this court adopting the latter as its guide..." 42 Fed. at 124, 127. While in Barry v. Mercein the Supreme Court dismissed the appeal on jurisdictional grounds without reaching the merits, the report of the argument, 46 U.S. at 104, 114, left no doubt both of the grounds for Judge Betts' decision and the array of authorities opposing Justice Story's assertion of jurisdiction in Green. In In Re Burrus, 136 U.S. 586, 591, 594 (1890), the Supreme Court, holding that "[i]t is not now the law, therefore, and never was, that every person held in unlawful imprisonment has a right to invoke the aid of the courts of the United States for his release by the writ of *habeas corpus*," expressly adopted Judge Betts' opinion as "very careful" and "very able" and printed it as an appendix to its own.

The second, and principal, precedent relied on by Judge McAllister was the decisions, less than a year before, of the United States District Court for the Eastern District of Pennsylvania in the *Case of Passmore Williamson*, which, together with those of the Pennsylvania Supreme Court in related proceedings, were widely available in book and pamphlet form in 1856.[124] These opinions of the Honorable John K. Kane, United States district judge, born of his deep-seated aversion to the combination of Quakers and slaves,[125] mark the greatest perversion of the writ of habeas corpus in the history of federal jurisprudence.

The case arose on the afternoon of July 18, 1855, aboard a steamer about to depart the Walnut Street dock in Philadelphia for New York. Passmore Williamson, the secretary of the Pennsylvania Abolition Society, approached the United States minister en route to his post in Nicaragua, Col. John H. Wheeler, and his slaves Jane and her two young sons, and told her that she and her children, having been brought into Pennsylvania, were free. A crowd of black people collected around Wheeler and Williamson, and Wheeler's slaves departed surrounded by the crowd.

Wheeler immediately secured from Judge Kane a writ of habeas corpus directing Williamson to produce Jane and her sons before the court, together with the grounds upon which Williamson detained them. On July 20 Williamson made a return in open court that the slaves were not, and had never been, in his custody, that he had not seen them since their disembarkation on July 18, and that he did not know their whereabouts. Williamson's request for a brief postponement being overruled, there followed a hearing at which Wheeler and several other witnesses testified that Wheeler's life had been threatened, and his slaves forcibly removed against their will, by the crowd surrounding him on the steamer. Williamson testified that Jane and her sons had willingly quit the steamer for their freedom, and that he had restrained only

CASE OF PASSMORE WILLIAMSON.

REPORT OF THE PROCEEDINGS

ON THE

WRIT OF HABEAS CORPUS,

ISSUED BY

THE HON. JOHN K. KANE,

JUDGE OF THE DISTRICT COURT OF THE UNITED STATES FOR THE EASTERN DISTRICT OF PENNSYLVANIA,

IN THE CASE OF

THE UNITED STATES OF AMERICA EX REL.

JOHN H. WHEELER vs. PASSMORE WILLIAMSON,

INCLUDING

THE SEVERAL OPINIONS DELIVERED;

AND

The Arguments of Counsel, Reported by Arthur Cannon, Esq., Phonographer.

PHILADELPHIA:
URIAH HUNT & SON, N. FOURTH STREET.
1856.

Title page of a printed account of the case of Passmore Williamson.

Wheeler, when he would not let go of Jane. He also testified that he knew but one of the people in the crowd, the clerk of the Anti-Slavery Office, who had earlier alerted him to the presence of Wheeler and his slaves aboard.

On July 27 Judge Kane found that Wheeler's slaves had been forcibly abducted by the crowd, that Williamson had acted in concert with them, and that therefore so much of his return on the writ that Wheeler's slaves had never been in his custody was false. He immediately committed Williamson to prison for contempt of court. A motion by Williamson's counsel to amend the return to strike the offending, basically irrelevant language was brushed aside by Judge Kane.

Applications made by Williamson's counsel in late July to the chief justice of the Pennsylvania Supreme Court, and in August to its full bench, for his release on the grounds that the district court had no jurisdiction to issue the writ of habeas corpus were denied, the state judges, with one impassioned dissent and one doubting concurrence, refusing to look beyond the existence of the committal for contempt. In October, counsel for Jane, safely in Massachusetts with her sons, tendered a petition sworn before the United States commissioner in Boston, confirming Williamson's July 20 testimony, denying that she or her children had been restrained of their liberty since breaking free of Wheeler's grasp aboard the steamer on July 18, and moving that the writ of habeas corpus be quashed. Judge Kane refused to receive her petition, dismissing Jane's sworn statement that she and her sons were not illegally restrained as probable "proof that the constraint is still effectual."

Late in October, with Williamson ill from his confinement in Moyamensing Prison, his counsel filed a new return, first as an affidavit and then as a petition for his release, but Judge Kane refused to entertain anything but an application by Williamson to purge himself of contempt. Having exacted this, on November 3 Judge Kane released Williamson, accepting what Williamson had vainly sought to proffer on July 27 by the amendment to his return.

Judge Kane's treatment of Williamson created a national furor, his critics and supporters dividing along sectional lines.[126] Jurisprudentially, however, Judge Kane's opinions were promptly recognized for the aberrations they were. In the third edition of his treatise on federal jurisdiction published in early 1856, Judge Alfred Conkling, then in his twenty-second year as United States district judge for the northern district of New York, had this comment, at the conclusion of his discussion of the jurisdictional limitation effected by the proviso in Section 14 of Judiciary Act of 1789:

> It seems, nevertheless, to have been altogether overlooked in a case of recent occurrence in the Eastern District of Pennsylvania, a case that has elicited no inconsiderable degree of public attention and interest. The proceedings I allude to, have been strongly marked throughout by features of a most extraordinary and anomalous character, and seem destined to occupy a conspicuous place in the judicial history of this country.[127]

The new edition of Judge Conkling's treatise was in Judge McAllister's hands when his opinion was written and a section of it, two pages earlier than that set out above, is quoted in his opinion.

Judge McAllister also found in the *Case of Passmore Williamson* the basis to allow M. des Rochers standing to sue out the writ of habeas corpus. The peculiarity of a litigant applying for a writ for his judge is not lessened by the fact that, despite the recital that des Rochers was plaintiff and the County of San Francisco defendant in an action argued and submitted at the January 1856 term of the Supreme Court of California, no record of the case has been found. The probable strategy behind the selection of such an applicant — for Mrs. Terry was in San Francisco[128] and would undeniably have been a proper party to apply for a writ of habeas corpus — was the use of des Rochers' status as an alien to provide an additional argument, under Section 11 of the Judiciary Act, for the presence of federal jurisdiction, a tactic repeated but rejected by the Court in *In Re Burrus, supra*, 136 U.S. at 595-96.

To support des Rochers' right to apply for the writ, Judge McAllister relied on Judge Kane's statement that "[t]he American books are full of cases - they are within the experience of every practitioner at the bar - in which the writ has issued at the instance of third parties, who had no interest or right in the matter than what man concedes to sympathy with the oppressed," adding his own comment that "[t]hese views are as sound law as they are eloquently expressed." However, Judge Kane's eloquence was employed in vaunting "sympathy with the oppressed" both as the pretext to sustain Wheeler's continued pursuit of Jane and her children, his slaves, by means of a writ of habeas corpus, and as the justification to refuse to consider her pleading, both more eloquent and more accurate, in support of quashing the writ:

> Because, under the writ of habeas corpus, which is a writ devised and intended to restore freemen to liberty when unduly restrained thereof, the said John H. Wheeler seeks to reclaim and recover your petitioner and her said children, and reduce them again into slavery.

As it turned out Judge McAllister's opinion proved an unnecessary tour de force. On August 6, after a joint meeting of the executive committee and the board of delegates, the views of the executive committee prevailed by a narrow vote. On August 7 Justice Terry was released after being read the verdict and recommendation that he resign his office.[129] Because of the dissatisfaction with the outcome on the part of many of the rank and file of the Vigilance Committee, for his own safety he was soon escorted aboard the *John Adams*.[130] Within a few days, he had resumed his seat on the California Supreme Court. At the conclusion of *Ex-Parte Des Rochers*, the reporter notes: "The writ was not served, the party in confinement having been released the night before the writ was to have been served."

On August 18, having concluded that their work was finished, the members of the Vigilance Committee held a final, triumphal parade through the streets of San Francisco. It was not only a parade of celebration but also one of warning, particularly to Judge McAllister and others involved in the federal criminal process. The case of Durkee and Rand was still pending, and while the Vigilance Committee had formally disbanded, its members had not gone far. The executive committee's communication to the general membership at the time made the point explicitly:

. . . your executive committee will endeavor themselves to exercise vigilance in the investigation and reformation of abuses, and in aiding and urging on the constituted authorites in the discharge of their duties, reserving the discretion and privilege of reassembling the board of delegates, or the general body, should serious occasion arise. Such occasion in the judgment of the executive committee might be found . . . upon the necessity of protecting any member of the Committee from violence or malicious prosecution, arising out of any act performed by authority of the Committee. . .[131]

Vigilance Committee parade through San Francisco, August 18, 1856. While marking the formal disbanding of the Vigilance Committee, this parade also indicated the extent of support for the committee three weeks before the trial of Durkee began. (Courtesy California State Library.)

VII

THE TRIAL OF JOHN L. DURKEE

Despite these warnings, on September 1 a grand jury was empanelled in the circuit court before Judges McAllister and Hoffman. The grand jury was, in Durkee's words, "packed [with] anti-Vigilance men,"[132] and Judge McAllister left little doubt what he expected of it:

> Judge McAllister delivered a charge to the jury, in which he dwelt particularly upon the recent state of affairs in San Francisco. He said that he would call the especial attention of the jury to the recent depredations committed upon the honor and dignity of the United States either here or at Sacramento, or at some intermediate point. He said that anybody engaged in those outrages against the United States must be considered as a principal in them, and that it would be the duty of the jury to investigate the matter. He required the jury to keep secret the counsel of the United States, and also their own counsel, and that they should present no one from fear or malice, &c.[133]

The press confidently predicted the indictment of Durkee and Rand.

Two days later Durkee and Rand were charged in separate indictments with piracy, specifically the boarding of the *Julia*, the assault of its crew, and the robbery of 113 muskets belonging to the State of California, "in the Bay of San Pablo within the ebb and flow of the sea..."[134] The indictment was laid under the Act of 1820, which provided for a mandatory death penalty upon conviction. No appeal lay from the judgment of the circuit court in a criminal case in the absence of a division of opinion between the two judges sitting.

Durkee and Rand surrendered to United States Marshal McDuffie's deputies and, represented by J.B. Crockett and William Duer, were arraigned in the circuit court the next day before Judges McAllister and Hoffman. The prosecution, as it had been before the grand jury, was represented by William Blanding, the United States district attorney for the Northern District of California, a South Carolinian who had fought in the Mexican War.

Crockett moved that the defendants be admitted to bail, emphasizing that they had been granted bail before and had surrendered to answer the indictment. Crockett also read the affidavit Durkee had filed in the earlier bail proceedings before Judge Hoffman, asserting that his admitted forcible taking of the arms from the *Julia* had occurred only to avoid the "armed collision, resulting in Civil War" that would have followed their delivery, and argued as a matter of law "that the facts of the case would in no wise warrant the finding of any intention to rob or steal or convert to their own use the property which had been taken by Rand, Durkee and the others, from the schooner *Julia*." His co-counsel, William Duer, speaking after United States District Attorney Blanding had voiced his opposition to the application, pointed out that "all

Authorized By No Law

John L. Durkee. This photograph was taken in 1893. (Courtesy California Historical Society, San Francisco.)

the facts were admitted and well known to the Court" and that "the offense was only *technically* an offense against the United States..."

The court adjourned for consideration of the motion, and, when it resumed at four o'clock that afternoon, bail was denied. Judge McAllister said:

> I am asked to exercise the discretion imposed upon me by law, on the ground that the act admitted to have been committed does not constitute a crime against the laws of the United States. Whether it does or does not constitute such crime, involves a deliberate examination of the law of felonious intention, as an element in the crime of larceny. To whatever conclusion I shall arrive on this question, important decisions of high judicial tribunals must be overruled. In advance of any discussion before me, it is due to the impartial administration of justice, that the great principles involved in this case should be disposed of, not summarily, but after a full hearing on the trial...

Durkee's trial was set for Monday, September 8.

Even General Sherman reacted cautiously to Judge McAllister's decision. That evening, in a letter to the St. Louis partners of Lucas, Turner & Co., he wrote:

> Judge McAllister has refused to bail Durkee on his Charge of Piracy and the Vigilance Committee have sent notices to all their armed forces to be in readiness at the call of their bell... I would not have the Judge to swerve one iota from the course he would pursue in times of quiet, but it would be well not to arouse these men who think they have saved the country from the control of rowdies. At the same time I don't see how we are to escape the necessity of putting down this spirit of resistance to the Law, for it will be repeated again and again until subdued by force or until some outrage causes the more peaceable inhabitants to rebel against the assumed authority of their Executive Committee.[135]

The proceedings on September 4 were published in detail in the next day's issue of the *San Francisco Daily Evening Bulletin*, James King of William's newspaper, now edited by his brother Thomas. The same issue carried a vitriolic denunciation of "the officers of the law" and speculated about, if it did not actually encourage, a return of the Vigilance Committee to put an end to the proceedings:

The Public Feeling.

> We have rarely seen so much feeling and unanimity of sentiment in this community, as has been exhibited for the last forty-eight hours, or since it became evident that the U.S. officers were in earnest in the farce they are engaged in at the Circuit Court, with the piracy case. The motives of the principal actors in this affair are so palpable and revolting to all good men that the feelings of the latter portion of the community are greatly outraged. Since

the refusal of the Court to admit the prisoners to bail, which is regarded as an indignity to the Committee and not as a matter of obedience to the laws or a fear of their escape from the jurisdiction of the Court, there has been but one sentiment entertained or expressed outside the little band of law and murder men, and that is a contempt for and an abhorrence of those men who will lend themselves and their official positions to this nefarious plan to bring the Federal Government in conflict with the people of this city.

We have met scores of men on the streets, in their stores, and shops, at their firesides and of every class in the community, who have heretofore stood aloof from the Committee, who now declare that they cannot be neutral any longer; and that if another demand is made for a call of "to arms," they will be found first and foremost in the ranks of the Committee. It has become now a matter of personal safety and self-preservation.

* * * *

The policy of the Executive is now, as it always has been to act with coolness and deliberation, and yet with resolution. They will not move in the present crisis until by insult, indignity and outrage they are compelled to; but when they do move let those who dare now to put the will of the people at defiance stand from under.

A separate editorial also characterized the highmindedness of the conduct of Durkee and Rand aboard the *Julia* and contrasted it with those involved in their prosecution:

To carry out their intentions, and to prevent bloodshed, it became necessary to disarm the rowdies who opposed them. For this purpose, and to carry out the common design, Durkee and Rand were sent to intercept and take possession of the muskets and munitions of (I had almost said war) murder *in transitu*, from the imbecile Governor to the miserable blacklegs enrolled under the banner of the ballot box stuffers, gamblers and assassins. In this, they were actuated by no desire of gain, avarice had not entered into their breasts; they sought not to take any man's property for their own use; they wished to deprive no person of what belonged to them; their motives were pure, high and noble. They accomplished their errand without bloodshed, without menace, without injuring the parties in charge. Was this the conduct of pirates? If they had been piratically inclined, would they not have thrown the worthless scoundrels overboard, agreeably to the piratical maxim of "dead men tell no tales?"

What is the consequence of this patriotic, disinterested act? What reward do they obtain for their heroic conduct? What influences and power put them where they now are?

Through the machinations of a few such wily, jesuitical scamps as Casserly, aided by such instruments as gambler McDuffie, upon the affidavit of one Phillips, a man now under indictment for felony, a fellow whose oath no decent man would believe, the ready Clerk of the U.S. Circuit Court issues a

> warrant for their arrest. The murderers fiendishly laugh at their success, they rub their hands in demoniac glee, they are about to be avenged for the loss of their kindred spirits, Casey and Mulligan!
>
> But lo and behold! the accused are admitted to bail, the Judge intimating that the charge could not be sustained. What should the hounds do now?
>
> The father of one of the rabid members of the law and murder clique arrives — he is a Judge — the chances brighten. A Term is convened. The gambler, with the aid of others of his party, pack a jury, and to avoid suspicion, put on it one or two respectable men. Now, I would ask, what show have Durkee or Rand?
>
> The *Judge*, the father of one man who volunteered and went to defend the jail, and aided and abetted the malicious and wicked purposes of the rowdy crew - the *Judge*, the father of another man who is sergeant at arms of a Club who pass resolutions denouncing the honest and virtuous of our citizens. The father-in-law of the *Judge's* son who defended the jail, is put on the jury. Could it be expected otherwise than that the honorable and manly would be indicted? Certainly not. Well, a true bill is found against them; a motion is made to admit to bail, and refused for the alleged reason (among others equally foolish) that only a few days intervene previous to the trial. Is this a reason why men should be confined in a prison? So far from it, humanity and justice would answer that it is the greater reason why they should be at liberty. Have they no witnesses to hunt up? Do they not require to consult with their counsel? Ought not every moment be afforded them to prepare for the ordeal they have to undergo? The refusal to admit to bail is pregnant with the spirit that dictated it. We can draw our own conclusions.

The atmosphere of menace was not without its effect on those conducting the trial. The same day these editorials appeared, Marshal McDuffie wrote to General Wool:

> Sir: I now hold under the process of the United States circuit court for this district two prisoners, Durkee and Rand, who have been indicted for piracy by the grand jury. It is a fact probably within your knowledge that these men are sustained by a large number of persons in this city, who avow their determination to protect them at all hazards. In view of this state of things there is reason to apprehend an attempt to rescue these prisoners from my custody. In such an event, it would be very desirable to have the aid of the forces subject to your orders, to protect the court in the execution of its process and maintenance of its authority.
>
> Will you be so good as to inform me how far I can rely on your cooperation, and how soon it may be obtained, if it should be needed.[136]

General Wool, after his experience with Governor Johnson and General Sherman, was not about to get drawn in easily, and put McDuffie off in his reply on September 6:

> ... it appears to me it would be time enough to say what I would or would not

United States District Court Judge Ogden Hoffman. With Judge McAllister, Judge Hoffman sat on the circuit court during the trial of Durkee. (Photograph by Jose Maria Mora, New York City; reproduced courtesy California Historical Society, San Francisco.)

do when the "court of this district" calls on me for a military force to protect it in the discharge of its duties. Until it does make the call, I can only refer you for a conclusive answer to your communication to the laws of the United States, which I think are too plain to be misunderstood.[137]

On September 8 the proceedings opened with a motion by Crockett to consolidate the indictments of Durkee and Rand for trial. Judge Hoffman announced his opinion against the motion, but Judge McAllister stated that the court had discretion in the matter and would take time to consider it if the defense wished to press it. When counsel stated that they did — asserting that each defendant at a joint trial would have a separate right to a full number of peremptory challenges — the court was adjourned until the morning of September 10.

While considering the motion, the judges also took time to write their own letter to General Wool at Benicia:

> CHAMBER CIRCUIT COURT UNITED STATES
> District of California, San Francisco,
> September 9, 1856.
>
> Sir: There are two prisoners in custody of the marshal of the United States against whom true bills for piracy have been returned by the grand jury. These men will be placed on trial on to-morrow, and the investigation will occupy some two or three days. The marshal reports that, with the force ordinarily at his command, he is unable to ensure the safe-keeping of the prisoners, or command respect for the process of the court. It is impracticable for us to ascertain in advance the issue of the trial. Under these circumstances we deem it proper to learn from you whether you have any orders which, in your opinion, will authorize you to extend any aid to the marshal for the purpose of maintaining the laws, in case an attempt shall be made to nullify the process of the court.
>
> We have the honor to be, very respectfully, your obedient servants,
>
> M. HALL McALLISTER,
> Circuit Judge United States.
> OGDEN HOFFMAN,
> District Judge.[138]

The next day, September 10, when court opened, Judge Hoffman read a lengthy opinion denying that the court had any power to consolidate the cases for trial. Judge McAllister expressed the view that the court did have discretion to do so, but in view of Judge Hoffman's opinion otherwise, he would agree that the defense motion should be denied. Jury empanelling began, Judge McAllister ruling that Durkee might exercise thirty-five peremptory challenges, rather than the twenty that U.S. District Attorney Blanding sought to limit him to. He also ruled that no member of the Vigilance Committee or the Law and Order party should serve on the jury.

While this was going on, General Wool's reply to the judges' letter was on its way to San Francisco. Thus finally put to the question, General Wool gave the judges the same answer he had given Governor Johnson and General Sherman three months before — he would not act. In his letter of September 10, after paraphrasing the judges' request, General Wool responded curtly:

> In reply, I have only to remark that I have no orders whatever applicable to the subject in question. I must refer you to the laws of the United States, by which I am totally governed.[139]

A few days before, one of the members of the executive committee, James Dows, had publicly voiced a threat which was fast approaching a potential reality: "if they [Durkee and Rand] were convicted, that Judge McAllister and the Jury, and the United States Marshal would be hung out the windows of the Court House."[140]

And so, on the afternoon of September 11, with jury selection complete, the taking of evidence began; it would last less than three hours. John Mannix, the master of the *Julia*, testified that ten or twelve men had boarded the vessel in San Pablo Bay between two and three o'clock on the morning of June 21 and, in the name of the Vigilance Committee, had transferred at gunpoint from her hold to their sloop the boxes containing the arms loaded at Benicia. McNabb and Phillips testified to the same effect, and each identified Durkee as one of the boarding party. General William C. Kibbe, Adjutant General of the California militia, testified to his frequent, recent and futile demands of the Vigilance Committee to return the state arms it still held.

Duer then opened to the jury, arguing that the arms had been taken "to prevent bloodshed...not... with an intention to steal; it was not a taking *animo furandi* [with intent to steal] and *lucri causa* [for the sake of gain], as the law expressed it." The defense called George R. Ward, a member of the executive committee, who testified that the muskets from the *Julia* had never been used and would be returned, in their original packages, at the appropriate time, provoking from Judge McAllister the sarcastic comment, "You mean that you will give them up, when you please to do so."

Summations were begun by U.S. District Attorney Blanding, followed by Duer and Crockett, and closing with Blanding's rebuttal. The arguments to the jury were devoted mainly to the necessary felonious intent for conviction, Blanding contending that "pecuniary gain to the person who took the property" was unnecessary, while the defense maintained that "an intention of stealing for the sake of gain" was required. Taking the opportunity to quote Justice Terry's praise of the committee when opening his defense at his own trial, Duer also suggested "that the objects of the Committee were noble ones, and hoped that the jury would restore peace to the city by a conscientious verdict; this case seemed to be the only matter of controversy left, and when settled, there would probably be quiet and peace."

At ten o'clock that night Judge McAllister charged the jury. After expressing his horror that bias or prejudice might play any part in the verdict — and directing the jury to disregard the suggestion that Durkee was acting on the orders of the Vigilance Committee, "which we charge you was unauthorized by and banded together in violation and defiance of the laws" — Judge McAllister told the jury, that whatever other crimes he might be guilty of, Durkee was on trial solely for piracy. This, the judge explained, was, under the Act of 1820, robbery on a vessel within the ebb and flow of the sea. To determine the meaning of that term, the court would look to the common law as it existed at the time of independence.

Judge McAllister charged that the crime of robbery depended on the intent which accompanied such a larceny by intimidation or force. He then reviewed at length a number of cases from state jurisdictions and from England, explaining that the requisite intent was lacking if either permanent deprivation of the property was not intended at the time of the taking or if the purpose of the taking was not for personal profit. Two later English cases to the contrary, relied on by the prosecution, were dismissed as against the weight of authority, rejected by English and American judges, and not to be considered because decided after American independence. Judge McAllister's last words to the jury were:

> But if you shall believe that he did not take the arms for the purpose of appropriating them, or any part thereof, to his own use, and only for the purpose of preventing their being used on himself or his associates, then the prisoner is not guilty.

The report of the trial says: "As soon as Judge McAllister's opinion was delivered a violent stamping and applause commenced among the audience..." It took the jury three minutes to bring in a verdict of acquittal. The U.S. district attorney immediately entered a nolle prosequi in the prosecution of Rand. The court discharged the prisoners and "then adjourned amidst the huzzas of the people, which were long and loud."

VIII
CONCLUSION

The application of the federal piracy statutes to domestic insurrections was no easy task for the federal courts. Judge McAllister was the first to be confronted with the problem, but, in October 1861, the Civil War forced Justices Samuel Nelson and Robert C. Grier, sitting in United States circuit courts in New York and Philadelphia, respectively, to address similar issues in the context of piracy prosecutions of captured Confederate privateers. There, of course, the defendants' principal contention was that the privateering commissions issued to their vessels by Jefferson Davis, president of the Confederate States, pursuant to statute provided a complete defense to the charge, while in the *Durkee* case it was argued that necessity, rather than any law, provoked the taking of the muskets from the *Julia*. However, in all three cases, to a lesser or greater extent, the application of traditional notions of felonious intent to forcible takings at sea for political reasons created an issue at trial which the court was obliged to address in its instructions and the jury, in following them, to consider in its deliberations.

It has been suggested that aspects of Justice Nelson's charge at the trial of the officers and crew of the schooner *Savannah*, including his instructions on intent, created sufficient ambiguity in the minds of the jury to prevent a verdict and that this result was consistent with the justice's political views and personal activities during the period between secession and the bombardment of Fort Sumter.[141] Just the opposite is true of the *Durkee* case.

Judge McAllister plainly thought and repeatedly said that the activities of what he called "the associated mobites styling themselves a Vigilance Committee" were illegal, and undoubtedly he was right; indeed, the committee admitted as much. Moreover, Judge McAllister had been an outraged witness to the consequences of the committee's actions while aboard the *John L. Stephens* in late June, and in late July he had stretched the law past the breaking point in an effort to extract Justice Terry from the committee's custody. In addition, Judge McAllister had invited the grand jury to indict Durkee and Rand on September 1, had refused them bail on September 4 and had agreed to deny their request for a joint trial on September 10.

In sharp contrast, Judge McAllister's charge to the jury on September 11 was neither ambiguous nor consistent with his antipathy to the Vigilance Committee. It was, instead, such an overt direction to acquit that the spectators stamped and cheered, the jury took but three minutes to bring in its not guilty verdict, and the court adjourned "amidst the huzzas of the people, which were long and loud."

It seems the decision that there should be an acquittal had been arrived at before any evidence had come in. The charge, delivered at ten o'clock at night after an afternoon in which all the evidence was taken and an evening filled with the summations of counsel, was far too complex and detailed to have been prepared to any significant degree during or after the testimony and argument preceding its delivery. It is evident from his remarks at the conclusion of the bail hearing on September 4 that Judge McAllister was perfectly aware of the admitted facts, of the legal issue on which the case would turn, and of the conflict of authorities bearing on that issue which would let him put the case to the jury as he chose.

The key to the outcome may be Judge McAllister's letter of September 9 to General Wool. No one intending to deliver the charge Judge McAllister would on September 11 could possibly have had any doubt of the outcome or reason even to inquire whether troops would be available to enforce the process of the court. But Judge McAllister did write the letter. Given the consistency of his opposition to the committee up to that time, the inference is fairly compelling that when he wrote to General Wool on September 9 Judge McAllister contemplated jury instructions of a radically different tenor than the direction to acquit he actually delivered on the 11th. Evidently, something happened between the 9th and the end of the trial to change his mind. Just as Commodore Farragut's gunboats had nerved Judge McAllister into granting the writ for Justice Terry, perhaps it was General Wool's letter of September 10, refusing to provide military aid in the event of a conviction, which determined what Judge McAllister's charge to the jury would be.

APPENDIX

Trial of United States v. John L. Durkee
Proceedings of September 4, 1856*
U.S. Circuit Court - Before Judges McAllister and Hoffman.

The cases of John L. Durkee and Charles E. Rand were called up. They had been indicted for piracy upon the high seas, and having surrendered themselves to the U.S. Marshal, were placed in custody.

At the opening of the Court, Col. Crockett said that he would make a motion to admit the accused to bail, but preliminary to it, he would ask the Court as to its view with regard to its power to admit the prisoners to bail.

Mr. Blanding, the U.S. District Attorney, said that he wished to say a word or two in relation to the subject. He said that he did not doubt but that the Court had the power to bail, though in his opinion the circumstances of the cases under consideration would not justify an admission to bail.

Colonel Crockett then proceeded to give the reasons why the accused should be admitted to bail. He said that he was glad the District Attorney had admitted the right of the Court to admit to bail, and that the only question therefore would be, whether the Court ought in the exercise of a sound discretion to grant the motion. He said that the facts of the case would in no wise warrant the finding of any intention to rob or steal or convert to their own use the property which had been taken by Rand, Durkee and others, from the schooner *Julia*. He said that the facts were stated in affidavits which had been made in a former application to admit Durkee to bail. He then read the affidavit of Durkee.**

---

* *San Francisco Daily Evening Bulletin*, September 4, 1856, p. 3; September 5, 1856, p. 2.

** Durkee's affidavit, printed in the June 28, 1856 edition of the *San Francisco Alta California*, reads in pertinent part:

> That on the ___ day of June, 1856, the said sloop Julia was on a voyage from the port of Benicia to the port of San Francisco, having on board thereof as freight, several boxes containing muskets and military accoutrements belonging to the State of California, which were destined for the use of troops then being drilled and organized as aforesaid. That anticipating an armed collision, resulting in Civil War, the said Committee ordered the deponent and other persons to seize the said weapons and accoutrements, before their arrival in San Francisco, and where ever the same might be found and when so seized, to bring the same to the City of San Francisco, and deliver them to the said Committee. That in pursuance of, and in obedience to said order, deponent went on board said sloop whilst lying at anchor in the Bay of San
> *[footnote continued on following page]*

Col. Crockett after reading the affidavit, proceeded to say that the question which arose, was whether the parties were not as much entitled to bail now, as they had been before, when Judge Hoffman of the U.S. District Court granted a motion of the same kind. He said that the offense had been committed under peculiar circumstances and that the element of larceny was wholly wanting.

The organization, under whose authority the accused acted, whatever may have been the illegality of its organization, was still a powerful military body, having several thousands of armed men. Even considering the organization as a determined rebellion against the Government, which it could not be called, it would hardly be a proper case for such a stringent exercise of legal discretion against individuals.

The great object was to secure the attendance of the accused, and there was no reason to suppose, if they should be admitted to bail, that they would not be forthcoming. They had already once before been bailed and were forthcoming. Everything tended to give assurances that they would again be forthcoming. The speaker then read a number of authorities from the law books. The authorities all went to show that the Court has the power, and should in proper cases exercise the authority of admitting to bail even after an indictment has been found for a capital crime.

The U.S. District Attorney then made an address to the Court, maintaining the proposition that though the Court had the power to bail, yet that it should not exercise it, as a great public crime had been committed. He mentioned a number of authorities in which motions of the kind had been refused. He said that he had no particular desire to prevent the prisoners from being bailed, but he considered it his duty to oppose the application. He did not think the case one of those in which bail should be allowed.

Judge Duer, the colleague of Col. Crockett in the defense, followed Mr. Blanding. He said that Col. Crockett had presented fully enough the merits of the application. He then spoke of judicial discretion and the proper exercise of it. The main point was whether the person to be bailed would be present to stand his trial. He thought there was no doubt about it in this case. The men who had committed the offence, or those who had employed them, were numerous and were all ready to stand a trial for what they had done. None of them would endeavor to escape. They were too numerous; their standing in the community was too high; and they were all willing to have the questions arising in the case settled. He said that many of the cases in which applications to bail had been refused, as cited by the District Attorney, were decided upon a view of them which could not exist in this case. In those cited, the facts were only known to the Grand Juries, and there was nothing of a mitigating character in the evidence so far as the court could know. In this case, however, all the facts were admitted and well known to the Court.

> Pablo, and by force and violence, and against the consent of the master of said sloop, seized the said muskets and accoutrements, and placing the same on another vessel brought them to the City of San Francisco, and delivered them to the said Committee in whose possession they yet remain.

He said that the offense was only *technically* an offense against the United States. It was a rising up against the government of the State of California, in the view of whose Courts the offence would be merely larceny or robbery, and could not be one of a heinous character. It was a political offence of the character of treason, &c., perhaps; it was not a case of the ordinary character of murder, &c.

Judge McAllister interrupted the speaker, and said that the Court had nothing to do with the political view of the matter. They could only look at the offense in a legal point of view.

Judge Duer said that he did not wish to be understood as bringing into the discussion the moral question of the offence; good men differed about it, and it would be worse than useless to raise the feelings.

The Court then intimated that they would render their decision upon the motion at 4 o'clock, to which time a recess was taken.

At 4 o'clock, the Court Room was crowded, and considerable excitement prevailed. Judge McAllister said:

> After an anxious inquiry, we have arrived at the conclusion that no instance is on record, in the annals of criminal jurisprudence, which would authorize the discharge of the prisoners on bail. The indictments were returned against them for a capital offense on yesterday; the case assigned immediately for trial for next Monday, the 8th inst., a period which would allow, to the strictest activity, time within which to summon a jury.
>
> I am asked to exercise the discretion imposed on me by law, on the ground that the act admitted to have been committed does not constitute a crime against the laws of the United States. Whether it does or does not constitute such crime, involves a deliberate examination of the law of felonious intention, as an element in the crime of larceny. To whatever conclusion I shall arrive on this question, important decisions of high judicial tribunals must be overruled. In advance of any discussion before me, it is due to the impartial administration of justice, that the great principles involved in this case should be disposed of, not summarily, but after a full hearing on the trial, to take place in three days time. My reasons for the conclusion to which I have arrived, will be referred to on a future occasion.

Judge Hoffman said: In concurring with the foregoing decision, I feel it incumbent upon me to refer to the circumstances under which I acted as Judge of the U.S. District Court when the prisoners heretofore were admitted to bail. They had then been arrested on the charge of piracy; but it was uncertain whether the Grand Jury would find a bill against them and when they could be tried. I think that I did right in admitting them to bail upon that occasion, and should under such circumstances do it again. But now the Grand Jury have found true bills against them, and their confinement can at any rate be but for a few days. The circumstances do not afford a good reason for admitting bail, and I therefore concur with Judge McAllister in refusing the motion.

The prisoners were remanded back into custody and shortly afterwards the crowd dispersed.

Proceedings of September 8, 1856*

At the opening of the Court this morning, it being understood that the trial of the piracy cases of John L. Durkee and Charles E. Rand were to commence, the Court Room was densely crowded. A large number of attorneys were within the bar, and many spectators in those parts of the room partitioned off for the audience.

The United States District Attorney stated that the case of John L. Durkee was set for to-day, but that under the provisions of the law, he was bound to furnish the opposite counsel with a list of the jurors summoned two days before the empannelment. He said that he had not been able to comply with the law in this case, as there had not been time to do it since the making up of the *venire*. If opposite counsel required the time allowed by the law, the case would have to be put off.

After some consultation, Col. Crockett rose, with the United States Statutes in his hand, and moved to consolidate the cases of Durkee and Rand, at the same time reading certain provisions of the law, in relation to joinder or consolidation in such cases.

Mr. Blanding said, that it would be for the benefit of the prisoners to have separate trials. If they were joined, the two together would only have the number of challenges allowed to one. He did not think it a matter of much importance, however, whether there was a joinder or not.

Col. Crockett said that the defendants would prefer to have but one trial.

Judge Hoffman delivered an opinion against the motion. Judge McAllister delivered an opinion, that the Court had a discretion to join the cases, and said that if counsel should press the matter, the Court would take time to consider and finally decide it.

The counsel for the prisoners said that they made the motion with the conviction that the accused would be entitled to their separate challenges, and insisted upon the motion. The Court took the question under advisement, and adjourned the jurors till Wednesday at 11 o'clock. The Court room was vacated, and the ordinary business, calling the civil calendar, taken up.

---

* *San Francisco Daily Evening Bulletin*, September 8, 1856, p. 2.

Proceedings of September 10, 1856

The motion to consolidate the trials of Durkee and Rand was denied. *United States v. Durkee*, 25 Fed. Cas. 939 (No. 15,008) (C.C. D. Cal. 1856). Jury selection commenced. Judge McAllister ruled that Durkee was entitled to thirty-five peremptory challenges.* He also ruled that membership in the Vigilance Committee or the Law and Order party was grounds for disqualification. Jury selection began.**

Proceedings of September 11, 1856***

Jury selection completed. Trial commenced.
Mr. William Blanding, the United States District Attorney, addressed the jury in some brief preliminary remarks. He said that he would rely upon the law of 1820, which provides for the offence of piracy within the body of a State, and makes the punishment of it death.

Testimony For Prosecution

John Mannix, being sworn, said: I follow the sea. I command the schooner *Julia*. I commanded it in June last. I was with the *Julia* on the bay of San Pablo on the morning of June 21st, between 2 and 3 o'clock in the morning. We were at anchor. A boat came alongside of my vessel, and boarded me, and some men came on board my vessel. There were ten or twelve came on, armed with Colt's revolvers. They examined the hold of the *Julia*; I objected to it; but they still took off the hatches. They got at a lot of arms in boxes in the hold, and broke one box open. There were six boxes, directed to Governor Johnson. They took them on board of the sloop *Malvina*, on which they came. I recognized two persons who came on board the *Julia*. Mr. Rand and Mr. Hutton. I did not recognize Mr. Durkee, I do not know him. I was taken prisoner, and was kept so until the vessel was discharged.
On cross-examination:
We took the arms on board at Fifth street wharf at Benicia, from a United States Government team. I made the contract for carrying the arms with Mr. Maloney, Mr. Phillips and others. The occurrence of taking the arms was in San Pablo Bay, fourteen or fifteen miles from San Francisco, and about three miles from the Contra Costa

---

* *San Francisco Daily Evening Bulletin*, September 10, 1856, p. 3.

** *San Francisco Daily Evening Bulletin*, September 12, 1856, p. 2.

*** *San Francisco Daily Evening Bulletin*, September 12, 1856, p. 1.

shore. It was a good way above Red Rock. When the men came aboard they asked me whether I made any resistance, and pointed pistols at me. I asked what they were. They said they were the Vigilance Committee. — Had I any freight? I said it was none of their business. They then took off the hatches and took the arms, after making us prisoners. I asked what authority they had for taking the arms. They said they would show me bye-and-bye; but they never did show me. They told me they came to take the arms by order of the Vigilance Committee. We had no other freight on board. They stove in a part of my boat; but they paid me for that afterwards.

In answer to the Court:

Where this occurred was within the ebb and flow of the tide.

In answer to the District Attorney:

The men represented themselves to be the Vigilance Committee. The arms have never been returned. It is all the same when I said that they were the Vigilance Committee and that they came by order of the Vigilance Committee. They said that they came by the order of the Committee and that they would show it to me, but they never did.

John G. Phillips being sworn, said: I was on the schooner *Julia*, on June 20th. last. I went on at Benicia. We had a head wind. We anchored at a point called by our captain San Pablo Point. We were hailed by a party in a boat, and I heard the party in the boat say to the captain of the *Julia* that they did not intend to harm him or anybody else; but they wanted to get the arms on the schooner. They boarded the vessel, and although the captain protested, they took off the hatches and took the arms which were in the hold and brought them to San Francisco. I was in charge of the arms. I received them from the orderly sergeant. They belonged to the United States Department at Benicia. I had a requisition to have the arms delivered to me. Maloney and I made the contract with Mannix to carry the arms. I recognized only one of the men who came on the *Julia*. It was Durkee. I knew him well. When the arms came to San Francisco, they were placed on a dray and taken up town, and I did not see them any more. I was on the vessel a prisoner when the boat came to the wharf. I asked Durkee by what authority he acted. He said by order of the Vigilance Committee, and read a written paper. There were six or eight men came on to the *Julia*; they were well armed. The arms belonged to the State of California when I got them at Benicia; previously they had belonged to the United States.

On cross examination: I was at the time a second lieutenant in a militia company called out by the Governor's proclamation. I was sent after the arms by Gen. Howard. I was to bring the arms to my superior officer, and deliver them. I was to use the best of my discretion as to where I should land them. I was told to take them wherever I could land them in safety. This was the instruction given me by Gen. Howard. I was ordered to bring them to San Francisco, if I could. I should have delivered them to General Howard, or whoever might be in command here. I belonged to Calhoun Benham's company. They were drilling at the time. They were called out by the Governor.

The counsel for defense then offered the proclamation of the Governor in evidence.

Phillips continued: The company I belonged to had been mustered into service. I did not know that the arms were to be used in an assault upon the Vigilance

Committee — not of my own knowledge. In my company it was not generally talked of that there would be a collision: it was generally talked of that our company should maintain the law. Maloney, who was with me on the *Julia*, talked something about going into camp; he said it would be a good thing.

On direct examination resumed: These arms were not for any company that I know of. They were to be delivered to whoever was in command. General Howard was under commission.

In answer to the Court: The arms were taken forcibly and against our remonstrances. The men who took them said they were a portion of the Vigilance Committee.

James McNabb, being sworn, said: I was on board the *Julia* on June 21st; we came to anchor off San Pablo Point; between 2 and 3 o'clock we were boarded, and a lot of boxes, containing arms, taken out of the hold of the *Julia* and brought to San Francisco. Mr. Durkee and Mr. Rand were on the *Julia*; I knew them. I went to Benicia on June 18th; sent there to assist Mr. Phillips to bring the arms down to this city. The arms were taken against my consent; I did not think it worth while to resist.

On cross-examination: I was in my berth when the *Julia* was boarded; I did not hear much said at the time; something was said about the Vigilance Committee; I was a lieutenant in Ashe's company; a company organized under the Governor's proclamation, and mustered into service. James R. Maloney is not in the city.

Patrick McGuire being duly sworn said: I am a soldier. I belong to the ordnance department of the United States at Benicia. I delivered the arms to Phillips on June 20th. 113 muskets, a sabre and two rifle bullet moulds. The muskets were worth over $10 a piece. There were six boxes directed to the Excellency, J. Neely Johnson, Governor of the State of California, Sacramento city. I was directed to deliver the arms by Col. Ripley.

On cross-examination: I received orders to deliver the arms to any person representing the State. Col. Ripley told me two men would call for them. Two men, Phillips and Maloney came for them and brought the Governor's receipt for the arms. I delivered them.

Gen. Wm. C. Kibbe being sworn, said: I do not know anything about the taking of the arms from the schooner *Julia*. Mr. Phillips was not employed by me. I am Quarter-Master and Adjutant-General in the service of the State. I would have been the legal custodian of the arms. I had been directed by the Governor to make a demand upon the Vigilance Committee for certain arms. I made a demand for some ordnance belonging to the First California Guard, and afterwards for muskets belonging to the State, but did not succeed in procuring them. Two or three weeks since, I gave the Vigilance Committee notice that the State arms were wanted for the service against the Indians in the North. Three of the members of the Committee called upon me and said the arms would not be returned then, and gave me the reasons why. The arms have never been delivered to me, who am the legal custodian of them. I do not know positively where the arms are now. I think they have not been returned to the Governor.

On cross-examination: I made a demand lately for all of the arms of the State, not for the 113 muskets specifically. The reason given by the Committee for not returning the arms was, that the proclamation of the Governor was still in force, and that they could not therefore deliver them at that time with safety to themselves.

The prosecution then gave notice that they rested the case.

Judge Wm. Duer then addressed the jury in relation to the character of the defense. He said that piracy was sea robbery, and that robbery required a putting the person robbed in fear, and then *stealing* property from him. He commented on the fact of two contending parties being in existence at the time the arms were taken, the Vigilance party and the law and order party. There was a conflict expected between the parties, and the arms were taken to prevent bloodshed. They were not taken with an intention to steal; it was not a taking *animo furandi* and *lucri causa*, as the law expressed it. There was a studious desire, on the part of the Vigilance Committee from the beginning, to avoid bringing the United States into the controversy, and the United States had been made a party on mere technical grounds. There was no offense against the General Government, and none intended; that was patent, and was well known and understood by all.

Testimony For Defense

George R. Ward, being sworn, said: I was on June 21st last one of the Executive Committee of the Vigilance Committee. The papers shown me are the Constitution of the Vigilance Committee and an Address of the Committee to the People. I was one of a Committee appointed to wait upon Gen. Kibbbe in relation to the arms of the State. We asked him whether he was in earnest about asking for the arms. He said "yes," and that the arms were to be sent into the interior of the State. We said it was unreasonable to be asked to give up the arms then, as the same state of things existed as had existed before. The Governor's proclamation was still in effect. We did not refuse to give up the arms. Gen. Kibbe is mistaken. It was only a question of time when we should give them up, but we did not refuse to give them up.

Judge McAllister: You mean that you will give them up, when you please to do so.

Mr. *Ward* continued: The arms received from the schooner *Julia* were sent away from the Vigilance Committee rooms the same day they were received. They were never used by the Committee; in fact, I will pledge myself that the identical arms in their original packages shall be delivered up in proper time. A demand was made for the arms; we did not refuse to give them up; but did not give them up. The packages of the 113 muskets are stored, and will be delivered unopened at the proper time. I decline stating where they are.

The Defense here closed, and the Prosecution stated that they had no more evidence to offer.

Arguments

Mr. Blanding opened the argument, and commenced speaking at 4 o'clock. He said that a *felonious intent* in taking property was necessary to constitute a Piracy under the statute. He said that he would contend that the taking in the case was a felonious taking. He said it was not necessary to be shown that there was an object of pecuniary gain to the person who took the property, and presented a number of authorities.

Judge Duer followed at half past 4 o'clock, and said that in an ordinary case he would not think it necessary to say anything in the way of comment upon the evidence adduced. But the case was one of importance, not only to the prisoners, but to the public. He then reverted to the power given to the general government to punish piracy, and the peculiarity and extraordinary character of the provision in relation to piracy within the limits of a State. He then spoke of the distinctive characters of larceny and robbery and commented at large upon the authorities.

It being then 5 o'clock the court took a recess.

The Court met again at half past six o'clock, and Judge Duer proceeded with his argument and comments upon the adjudicated cases. The purport of his remarks was that it required an *animus furandi* and *lucri causa* (an intention of stealing for the sake of gain) to make a larceny, which in this case was a necessary ingredient in the crime of piracy. He concluded his remarks eloquently; spoke of the notable remarks of Judge Terry, that the objects of the Committee were noble ones, and hoped that the jury would restore peace to the city by a conscientious verdict; this case seemed to be the only matter of controversy left, and when settled, there would probably be quiet and peace.

Col. Crockett followed, and commented upon the authorities cited by the prosecution, and especially upon the celebrated "Bean Case."

The most important case for his side, cited by the District Attorney, was an English one, in which several servants, with a false key, entered their master's granary, and took two bushels of beans, with which they fed their master's horses. An English Court ruled that this taking of the beans was a larceny. The speaker showed that the doctrine of this case had been repudiated in the United States, and that Dickens, the celebrated novelist, who had done more than any other living man to liberalize the public character of England, had ridiculed and justly ridiculed it, in one of his latest publications. The only other case relied on by the District Attorney, was another English case, in which a man, who had backed a horse into a coal pit, and thereby killed him, was found guilty of a larceny of the horse. There was no intention, on the part of the man, to make advantage, in the way of gain, to himself, but merely to destroy the horse, which was evidence against a friend in a prosecution for burglary. The doctrine in this old English case, was also ridiculed in the more liberal jurisprudence of the present day.

Mr. Blanding commenced his concluding argument at 9 o'clock. He said that the proposition of the Vigilance Committee to give up the arms on condition of the withdrawal of the Governor's proclamation could not affect the case. He also cited law cases to show that an offer of restitution of the property could not affect the offense. He showed that the bean and horse cases had been cited with approval by late judges in England, and by Mr. Greenleaf, in his work on Evidence. Mr. Blanding concluded at 10 o'clock, when Judge McAllister charged the jury.

The charge was a long and very able exposition of the law upon the subject of piracy. It reviewed the various adjudicated cases, and those particularly which had been quoted in the arguments. We are not able to give it to-day; but we may state that he excluded the beans and horse cases of England on the ground that they had been adjudicated in England since the separation of the American colonies from the mother country. Up to 1776, the law of England had uniformly been that a taking must be *lucri causa et animo furandi* to constitute larceny or, in a case of this kind, piracy. He concluded with the direction to the jury that if they believed, from the evidence, that the prisoner took the arms with the intent to appropriate them to his own use, and permanently deprive the owner of them, then, in the opinion of the Court, he was *guilty*. But if they believed that he did not take the arms for the purpose of appropriating them to his own use, and only for the purpose of preventing them being used on himself or his associates, then he was *not guilty*!

As soon as Judge McAllister's opinion was delivered a violent stamping and applause commenced among the audience, but it was immediately suppressed. The jury went out and in three minutes returned to Court. Before their verdict was received, Judge McAllister addessed the crowd, which literally choked up the court room, and said that he hoped order would be preserved, and the dignity of the Court respected. Charles J. Brenham, foreman of the jury, then, in answer to a question by the clerk, said that the prisoner was "Not Guilty." The repressed feelings of the audience, notwithstanding the reproof of the Court, and the order that any one applauding should be arrested, here burst forth in loud hurrahs and clapping of hands.

The District Attorney then rose and addressed the Court as follows:

May it please the Court, it seems to me that there is no reason to prosecute this matter any further against Charles E. Rand, who is accused of precisely the same offense with which Durkee was accused. There is no reason why the Court should change its views, and I do not think that any new facts could be presented. The jury which has just returned a verdict has been, I am disposed to believe, an impartial one. I therefore, with the consent of the Court, will enter a *nolle prosequi* in the case of Rand.

Col. Crockett: May it please the Court, I move that the prisoners be discharged.

The Court: The prisoners are discharged.

The Court then adjourned admidst the huzzas of the people, which were long and loud.

Note: The charge to the jury is reported as *United States v. Durkee*, 1 McAllister's Reports 196, 25 Fed. Cas. 941 (No. 15,009) (C.C. D. Cal. 1856).

The following abbreviations are used for texts cited frequently:

15 American State Trials	J.D. Lawson (ed.), *15 American State Trials* (St. Louis, 1926)
Bancroft	H.H. Bancroft, *Popular Tribunals*, Vol. II (San Francisco, 1887)
Ex. Doc. 101	Executive Document No. 101, 34th Congress, 1st Session, U.S. Senate (Washington, 1856)
Ex. Doc. 43	Executive Document 43, 34th Congress, 3rd Session, U.S. Senate (Washington, 1857)
McAllister	W. McAllister, *Society as I Have Found It* (New York, 1890)
Nunis	D.B. Nunis, Jr., *The San Francisco Vigilance Committee of 1856* (Los Angeles, 1971)

Notes

1. An interesting and attractive account of a case tried in that court in 1861 may be found in B. McGinty, *Haraszthy at the Mint* (Los Angeles, 1975).
2. See, e.g., J.D. Gordan, III, "The Trial of the Officers and Crew of the Schooner 'Savannah' ", Supreme Court Historical Society Yearbook (1983), 31.
3. 1 Stat. 73.
4. 26 Stat. 826.
5. 1 Stat. 333.
6. 2 Stat. 89.
7. 2 Stat. 132, 156.
8. W. Holt, " '[I]f the Courts have firmness enough to render the decision:' Egbert Benson and the Protest of the 'Midnight Judges' Against Repeal of the Judiciary Act of 1801", in *Egbert Benson First Chief Judge of the Second Circuit (1801-1802)* (New York, 1987).
9. 9 Stat. 521.
10. 10 Stat. 161.
11. 9 Stat. 631.
12. *Cong. Globe*, 33d. Cong., 2d. Sess., 581-583, 604-608, 680-81, 971 (1855).
13. *Id.* at 604-605.
14. 10 Stat. 631.
15. 9 *Journal of Executive Proceedings of the Senate of the United States* (1969 reprint), 426.
16. *Id.* at 428.
17. XI *Dictionary of National Biography* (New York, 1933), 546; McAllister 5-6, 19. Substantial additional biographical information about Judge McAllister and his family may be found in a series of articles by Thomas Gamble in the *Savannah Sunday Morning News* in late 1930 and early 1931, available at the California Historical Society, San Francisco.
18. McAllister, 19.
19. McAllister, 20.
20. McAllister, 22.
21. McAllister, 24.
22. McAllister, 20, 25.
23. *Dictionary of National Biography, supra* note 17.
24. McAllister, 20.
25. McAllister, 26.
26. C.B. Swisher, 5 *History of the Supreme Court of the United States: The Taney Period 1836-64* (New York, 1974), 806.
27. *Ibid.* n. 161.
28. 12 Stat. 794.
29. 11 Stat. 6.
30. Nunis, 38.
31. See R.M. Senkewicz, S.J., *Vigilantes in Gold Rush San Francisco* (Stanford, 1985); P.R. Decker, *Fortune and Failures: White-Collar Mobility in Nineteenth-Century San Francisco* (Cambridge, 1978). The statements in the text do not represent in every particular the views of both authors.
32. Senkewicz, *supra* note 31, 5-6.
33. Cora's trial is reported in 15 American State Trials 16.
34. Senkewicz, *supra* note 31, 7-8. Bancroft, 35-40.

35. Bancroft, 47-50, 58-60.
36. Bancroft, 64-72; Nunis, 31-32.
37. Nunis, 32.
38. Bancroft, 97, 110-113.
39. Nunis, 150-52; Bancroft, 168-170.
40. Nunis, 33-35, 152.
41. Nunis, 153.
42. Nunis, 153; Bancroft, 183-192.
43. Bancroft, 228-233.
44. Nunis, 96-97; Bancroft, 235-237.
45. Bancroft, 292-93.
46. Bancroft, 293.
47. Nunis, 55; Ex. Doc. 101, 20.
48. Nunis, 55-56; Ex. Doc. 101, 3; Ex. Doc. 43, 26-27.
49. Nunis, 56; Ex. Doc. 43, 5; Bancroft, 295.
50. Ex. Doc. 43, 4.
51. Ex. Doc. 43, 3-5.
52. Ex. Doc. 43, 27-28; Nunis, 59.
53. Ex. Doc. 43, 5-6.
54. Nunis, 56-58; Ex. Doc. 43, 28-29; Bancroft, 305-10.
55. Bancroft, 320-323.
56. Ex. Doc. 43, 6-7.
57. Ex. Doc. 101, 2-4.
58. Ex. Doc. 101, 7-13.
59. Ex. Doc. 101, 15.
60. See Appendix.
61. Statement of John L. Durkee on the Vigilance Committee in San Francisco (1878), Bancroft Library.
62. File in United States v. John L. Durkee (Archives of the United States District Court, Northern District of California).
63. Nunis, 59-60.
64. The account in these last three paragraphs is taken from the testimony of the prosecution's witnesses at the trial of Justice Terry before the executive committee, cited *infra* at note 97.
65. Bancroft, 380-386.
66. Bancroft, 387-391.
67. Bancroft, 402, 437.
68. Bancroft, 404.
69. Bancroft, 405.
70. Ex. Doc. 101, 21-23.
71. Ex. Doc. 101, 23-24.
72. Ex. Doc. 101, 26-27.
73. Ex. Doc. 101, 25-26.
74. Ex. Doc. 101, 24.
75. Ex. Doc. 101, 17.
76. Ex. Doc. 101, 18-19.
77. Ex. Doc. 101, 28-29.
78. Ex. Doc. 101, 29-30.
79. L. Farragut, *The Life of David Glasgow Farragut, First Admiral of the United States Navy* (New York, 1879), 181-83.

80. *Id.* at 184.
81. See notes 61 and 62.
82. See note 62.
83. In 1857 Molony initiated a civil action for $100,000 damages in the New York Court of Common Pleas against two members of the executive committee who had traveled to New York. Although the decisions of the court on a preliminary procedural point and dismissal after trial for lack of jurisdiction are reported, *Molony v. Dows*, 15 Howard's New-York Practice Reports 261 (1858), 8 Abbot's Practice Reports 316 (1859), neither opinion provides much information about the evidence in the case. Through the kindness of Mrs. Sieglinde Rothschild and Mrs. Nancy Joseph, I have been able to examine the legal papers of Charles O'Conor, the eminent trial lawyer who acted for the defense, which are preserved at the New York Law Institute; these include the printed record, styled "Case," which contains the text of the testimony and the exhibits. References to that document hereafter are abbreviated "Case".
84. Case, 15-16.
85. Case, 44.
86. See note 62.
87. Case, 17-18.
88. Case, 18.
89. See Note 62.
90. Ex. Doc. 101, 22-23.
91. See note 62.
92. Bancroft, 504.
93. Case, 45-48.
94. Bancroft, 504.
95. *Barque Yankee v. Gallagher*, 1 McAllister's Reports 467, 469-70, 30 Fed. Cas. 781, 782 (No. 18,124) (C.C. D. Cal. 1859), *aff'g Gallagher v. The Yankee*, 9 Fed. Cas. 1091 (No. 5,196) (N.D. Cal. 1859). Judge McAllister affirmed Judge Hoffman's award of $3000 against the vessel which had carried Gallagher to the Sandwich Islands. As will be seen, *infra* n.96, Duane would ultimately fare less well.
96. While the incident involving Duane on the *John L. Stephens* is mentioned in Bancroft (at 598-600) and the indignation of an unnamed "high official" is briefly reported, Judge McAllister's identity and substantial participation in the incident go unmentioned. The information reported in this chapter comes from the record of litigation which Duane commenced against Captain Pearson (*Duane v. Pearson*) in the United States District Court in San Francisco, to which he returned in 1860 after countless travails once redeposited in Acapulco by the *Sonora*. It is one of the singularities of the case that Captain Pearson was represented by Hall McAllister, Judge McAllister's son and Duane's companion at the San Fransico jail.

In all Duane filed three libels in the District Court in July and August, 1860: one against the master of the tug *Hercules*, on which he had been carried out to the *Golden Gate* by the Vigilance Committee (*Duane v. Goodall*), one against the captain and first mate of the *Golden Gate* (*Duane v. Watkins and Walker*) and *Duane v. Pearson*. A stipulated judgment of two thousand dollars was entered in Duane's favor in *Duane v. Watkins and Walker* on November 20, 1861. After a trial at which Sterling Hopkins testified that it was he who had been in charge of Duane on the *Hercules*, Judge Hoffman dismissed the libel against its master on the ground that he was a joint tortfeasor with Watkins and Walker and Duane's settlement with them barred his action against Goodall. *Duane v. Goodall*, 7 Fed. Cas. 1132 (No. 4,105) (N.D. Cal. 1863).

The case against Pearson has a more interesting development. It was first tried in the District Court in October, 1863, and on December 2, 1863, Judge Hoffman, in an unreported opinion, found for Duane in the sum of four thousand dollars. An appeal was taken to the circuit court, and on June 21, 1864, eight years to the day after the seizure of the *Julia* and the arrest of Justice Terry, the case was retried before Justice Stephen J. Field on the record of the district court proceedings and the live testimony of six witnesses, including Duane and Pearson, the latter not having appeared at the trial before Judge Hoffman. On August 22, 1864, the circuit court, Field and Hoffman, JJ., sitting, affirmed the judgment of the district court. Pearson appealed to the Supreme Court, which unanimously remanded the case to the circuit court with directions to enter judgment in Duane's favor for fifty dollars only. *Pearson v. Duane*, 71 U.S. 605 (1866).

The narrative of this chapter follows and quotes the testimony of Duane in the district court, which was fully credited by Judge Hoffman and, in the district court, uncontradicted. Captain Pearson's testimony, first presented in the circuit court, denied that sympathy with the Vigilance Committee had had any role in the events on the *John L. Stephens*. Instead, according to Captain Pearson, he had returned Duane to Acapulco only because he was a stowaway, no offer having been made to pay Duane's fare. This testimony cannot have been much help to Pearson's cause, for his purser had testified that he had been under instructions to accept no fares for Vigilance Committee exiles, and Hall McAllister was also put in the unenviable position of having to stipulate that, if called, his father would have contradicted his client by affirming his offer to pay Duane's fare.

97. The record of the trial of Justice Terry was first published in pamphlet form on September 2, 1856 by one of the members of the executive committee, Bancroft 485; it is also reported in 15 American State Trials 125. References to the record, hereafter abbreviated "Terry Trial", are to the 1856 pamphlet.
98. Terry Trial, 3.
99. Terry Trial, 3-17.
100. Terry Trial, 17-20.
101. Terry Trial, 23.
102. Terry Trial, 22-23.
103. Terry Trial, 20-21.
104. Terry Trial, 21-22.
105. Terry Trial, 24.
106. Terry Trial, 24-25.
107. *Ibid.*
108. Terry Trial, 26.
109. Terry Trial, 27.
110. Terry Trial, 25, 26, 28.
111. Terry Trial, 32, 63.
112. Terry Trial, 36.
113. Terry Trial, 73. There is no mention of the guilty verdict on the assault on Purdy in the 1856 report, apparently because the board of delegates subsequently ordered the charge expurged from the record. A.R. Buchanan, *David S. Terry of California: Dueling Judge* (San Marino, 1956), 65-66.
114. Bancroft, 468-470.
115. A.E. Wagstaff, *Life of David S. Terry* (San Francisco, 1892), 120.
116. L. Farragut, *supra* note 79, 185-186.
117. Nunis, 157. The case referred to is one brought by Sherman's banking house, Lucas Turner & Co., to collect warrants issued by the City of San Francisco for the grading of Powell Street. The case was first decided at the October, 1856 term, but not reported. On rehearing, the court was unanimous in reversing the decision below adverse to Lucas, Turner & Co., but only Chief Justice Murray and Justice Terry were prepared to sustain Lucas, Turner & Co.'s position in full. *Lucas, Turner & Co. v. City of San Francisco*, 7 Cal. 463 (1857).
118. *Ex-Parte Des Rochers*, 1 McAllister's Reports 68, 7 Fed. Cas. 537 (No. 3,824), (C.C.D.Cal. 1856).
119. Although Judge McAllister's opinion is undated and the court file has not been located, this recital suggests the possibility that the petition was prepared after the action of the board of delegates on July 31.

120. 26 Fed. Cas. 30 (No. 15,256).

121. *Case of Passmore Williamson. Report of the Proceedings on the Writ of Habeas Corpus, issued by The Hon. John K. Kane, Judge of the District Court of the United States for the Eastern District of Pennsylvania, in the case of The United States of America ex rel. John H. Wheeler vs. Passmore Williamson* (Philadelphia, 1856); 28 Fed. Cas. 682, 686 (Nos. 16,725, 16,726) (E. D. Pa. 1855).

122. 8 Fed. Cas. 493 (No. 4,366). See also W. Rawle, *A View of the Constitution of the United States of America* (2d ed.: Philadelphia, 1829), 119.

123. A. Conkling, *A Treatise on the Organization and Jurisdiction of the Supreme, Circuit and District Courts of the United States* (2d ed.: New York, 1842), 92.

124. See note 120.

125. E.g., *Report of the Trial of Castner Hanway* (Philadelphia, 1852). R.L. Eckert, "Antislavery Martyrdom: The Ordeal of Passmore Williamson", *Penn. Magazine of Hist. and Biog.* 521, 526 n.16 (1976), states that Williamson himself had had an earlier run-in with Judge Kane in a case in Wilkes-Barre. The August 28, 1855 edition of the *N.Y. Herald Tribune*, which called for Judge Kane's impeachment, reported that Williamson had been active in an action for damages, and a prosecution for assault with intent to kill, brought two years earlier in Wilkes-Barre by a black, William Thomas, against three deputy U.S. marshals.

126. Eckert, *supra* note 125, at 533-35.

127. A. Conkling, *A Treatise on the Organization Jurisdiction and Practice of the Courts of the United States* (3d ed.: Albany, 1856), 79n.

128. Bancroft, 424.

129. Bancroft, 471.

130. Bancroft, 471-477.

131. Bancroft, 526-540.

132. See note 61.

133. The proceedings in court concerning the finding of the indictment against Durkee and his trial, as reported in the *San Francisco Daily Evening Bulletin*, are to be found in the Appendix.

134. See note 62.

135. William T. Sherman and Henry Turner Correspondence, 1854-59, 1872-78: Letter of William T. Sherman dated September 4, 1856, pp. 3-4 (New York Public Library, Microfilm reference number *ZL-175). A portion of this letter is reprinted in D.L. Clarke, *William Tecumseh Sherman: Gold Rush Banker* (San Francisco, 1969), 238.

136. Ex. Doc. 43, 10.

137. Ex. Doc. 43, 11.

138. Ex. Doc. 43, 11-12.

139. Ex. Doc. 43, 12.

140. Case, 28.

141. See note 2.

About the Author

John D. Gordan, III is a partner in the firm of Lord, Day & Lord. A graduate of Harvard College and of Harvard Law School, he has written frequently on the history of the federal courts and has published in the Supreme Court Historical Society *Yearbook*.